On-Site: NEW ARCHITECTURE IN SPAIN

On-Site: NEW ARCHITECTURE IN SPAIN

TERENCE RILEY

The Museum of Modern Art, New York

Published on the occasion of the exhibition
On-Site: New Architecture in Spain, at The Museum of
Modern Art, New York, February 12–May 1, 2006,
organized by Terence Riley, The Philip Johnson Chief
Curator of Architecture and Design.

The exhibition is the fourth in a series of five exhibitions
made possible by The Lily Auchincloss Fund for
Contemporary Architecture and is also made possible by
a generous grant from Enerfin Enervento, SA.

Major support is provided by PromoMadrid S.A., Madrid
Regional Ministry of Economy and Technological Innovation.

Additional funding is provided by Arcelor, by the
New York State Council on the Arts, a State Agency, by
MPG [Media Planning Group], by The Contemporary
Arts Council of The Museum of Modern Art, and by
The Consulate General of The Netherlands in New York.

This publication is made possible by Elise Jaffe + Jeffrey Brown.

Produced by the Department of Publications
The Museum of Modern Art, New York
Edited by Libby Hruska
Designed by Hsien-Yin Ingrid Chou
Production by Marc Sapir

Printed and bound by Dr. Cantz'sche Druckerei
Ostfildern, Germany
Typeset in Lisboa, General, and Knockout
Printed on 170 gsm Lumisilk

Library of Congress Control Number: 2005937778
ISBN: 0-87070-499-0

Published by The Museum of Modern Art
11 West 53 Street, New York, NY 10019-5497
www.moma.org

Distributed in the United States and Canada by D.A.P./
Distributed Art Publishers, Inc., New York

Distributed outside the United States and Canada by
Thames & Hudson, Ltd, London

Front cover: Felipe Artengo Rufino, Fernando Martín Menis,
and José M. Rodríguez-Pastrana Malagón with Mariola
Merino Martín | AMP Arquitectos. Athletics Stadium, Santa
Cruz de Tenerife

Back cover: Jean Nouvel | Ateliers Jean Nouvel with b720
Arquitectos. Torre Agbar, Barcelona. 2005. Lighting design
by Yann Kersalé

Printed in Germany

Photograph Credits

© Abalos&Herreros: 168–72; © Acebo X Alonso Arquitectos:
100–02; © Adam Woolfitt/CORBIS: 26 bottom; Fernando
Alda: 55, 57 top, 58–59, 95 top; © Álvaro Siza 2 Arquitecto
LDA: 54, 56, 57 bottom; Felipe Artengo Rufino, Fernando
Martín Menis, José M. Rodríguez-Pastrana Malagón, and
Mariola Merino Martín: cover, 134–36, 137 bottom, 138 top
and middle, 139 bottom; © Aranguren&Gallegos: 110–15;
Archive Photographique François Kollar, Paris: 8; Oscar
Barrio: 173; Berliner Bild Bericht, Berlin. The Museum of
Modern Art, New York: 28 left; Francisco Cabrero: 19 top;
© Carlos Alvarez/Getty Images: 27 top; Francesc Català-
Roca: 29 top; Cloud 9 with Acconci Studio and Ruy Ohtake:
104–09; Juan de Dios Hernández and Jesús Rey/Aurofoto:
199 top, 235 bottom; © Dominique Perrault Architecture:
116–19, 120 right, 121; Erika Ede © FMGB Guggenheim
Bilbao Museoa: 15; © Eisenman Architects: 48–52; © EMBT
Miralles Tagliabue Arquitectes Associats: 242, 243 middle
and bottom, 244–45; © Estudio Arquitectura Campo Baeza:
76–81; Jose María Flores: 75 bottom left and right; Kay
Fingerle: 28 right; © Foreign Office Architects (FOA): 70–74,
75 top; Javier Fresneda, Javier Sanjuan, Javier Peña: 252–57;
Valentín García Baca: 98 bottom, 99 bottom; © Gehry Partners, LLP: 122–27; Manuel González Vicente: 53; © Guallart
Architects: 150–55; © Guillermo Vázquez Consuegra:
156–61; © Roland Halbe: back cover, 36–41, 82–87, 128–33,
174–79, 222–27, 268–73; Heinrich Helfenstein: 14 bottom;
© Herzog & de Meuron: 16 bottom, 17, 162–67; © irisarri +
piñera: 216–21; © J.MAYER H.: 60–65; Lourdes Jansana: 243
top right; © José Maria Torres Nadal: 204–09; © Josep
Lluís Mateo – MAP Arquitectos: 186–91; © Juan Domingo
Santos: 94, 95 bottom, 96–97, 98 top, 99 top; © Juan Navarro
Baldeweg: 199 bottom, 200 top, 201–02; © Kazuyo Sejima +
Ryue Nishizawa/SANAA: 144–49; Francisco Leiva Ivorra and
grupo aranea: 180–85; © Diego Lezama Orezzoli/CORBIS:
20; Duccio Malagamba: 14 top; © Mangado y Asociados:
234, 236, 237 bottom, 238 top, 239; Mangado y Asociados
and Chroma: 235 top, 237 top, 238 bottom; © Mansilla+
Tuñón, Arquitectos: 42–47; © manuel bailo + rosa rull:
66–69; © MGM Morales+Giles+ Mariscal: 258–61; Enric
Miralles: 240; André Morin: 120 left; © Morphosis: 262–67;
© NO.MAD Arquitectos: 140, 141 bottom, 142 bottom left,
bottom right, 143 bottom; © Office for Metropolitan Architecture (OMA): 29 bottom, 192–97; Enrique Ojeda: 19 bottom;
Carlos Pesquiera: 198, 200 bottom, 203; Eugeni Pons: 22;
© Rafael Moneo: 12 top; © RCR Arquitectes: 16 top, 228–30,
231 top, middle, and bottom right, 232–33; Juan Rodriguez:
103; César San Millán/Mangado y Asociados: 27 bottom;
Oliver Schuh/Barbara Burg, Palladium Photodesign: 12
bottom; © selgascano: 246–51; Hisao Suzuki: 10, 26 top, 30,
137 top, 138 bottom left and right, 139 top, 141 top, 142 top
left, 143 top, 231 bottom left; © Toyo Ito & Associates, Architects: 88–93; © Adam Woolfitt/CORBIS: 26 bottom; © Zaha
Hadid Architects: 210–15; Rafa Zuza Elosegi: 241

Contents

Foreword

In 1929, the founding year of The Museum of Modern Art, the city of Barcelona played host to the World's Fair, bringing the talents of many international design professionals to Spanish soil for the first time. Ludwig Mies van der Rohe's masterful Barcelona Pavilion, dismantled after the exhibition and rebuilt fifty-seven years later, remains the seminal vestige of that event. In 1932, the Museum staged its first exhibition of architecture, which would become known as the International Style show, organized by Henry-Russell Hitchcock and Philip Johnson. Among the forty projects featured in the exhibition, just one was in Spain: José Maria Labayen and Joaquin Aizpuria's Club House in San Sebastián. In an opening text to the exhibition's catalogue, the curators remarked that in Spain "really modern architecture has only begun to appear."

The importance of Spain as a center of international design experimentation and excellence can further be traced in a 1966 exhibition celebrating Antoni Gaudí's landmark Sagrada Familia in Barcelona. In more recent years, exhibitions featuring the works of pivotal Spanish architects, including Santiago Calatrava, Enric Miralles, and Abalos&Herreros, have shown the country to be the home of some of architecture's most important voices. Today, the incredible wave of construction in Spain draws upon the talents of its own designers as well as the expertise of professionals from abroad.

The fifty-three projects presented in *On-Site: New Architecture in Spain*, organized by Terence Riley, The Philip Johnson Chief Curator of Architecture and Design, represent some of the finest examples of the diverse panorama of projects found throughout the country. Ranging from a handful of single-family homes to a new international airport for the city of Madrid, the exhibition highlights superior designs regardless of typology, scale, or budget. Mies's Barcelona Pavilion, with its rich but minimal material and compositional elegance, seems for many of the practitioners working in Spain today to be a vivid reference point. For others, this canon of modernism is simply the launching point for radical experimentation. Seen together, these projects, all but one of which have been or will be completed in the new millennium, provide a thoroughly up-to-the-minute look at Spain and its architecture.

Following *The Un-Private House*, *Tall Buildings*, and *Groundswell: Constructing the Contemporary Landscape*, *On-Site: New Architecture in Spain* is the fourth in a series of five exhibitions sponsored by the Lily Auchincloss Fund for Contemporary Architecture. We thank them for their continued support of this excellent program. We are also grateful to Elise Jaffe and Jeffrey Brown for their support of the publication. Equally, we are grateful to Terence Riley for his insightful essay and commitment to exploring new developments in contemporary architecture.

GLENN D. LOWRY
DIRECTOR, THE MUSEUM OF MODERN ART

Preface

Spain entered modernity with two pavilions. Ludwig Mies van der Rohe built the Barcelona Pavilion—a modern manifesto amid Beaux-Arts eclecticism—when that city hosted the International Exposition in 1929. And for the 1937 International Exposition in Paris, Josep Lluís Sert designed the Pavilion of the Spanish Republic, a white-walled Corbusian structure for which Pablo Picasso's *Guernica* was commissioned. Two years later both Mies and Sert would be living in the United States, having fled the turmoil of a continent where totalitarian rule was on the rise and war loomed on the horizon. *Guernica*, Picasso's cry of protest against the brutality of the fascist allies in Spain's civil war, was in exile, too, having been deposited by the artist with The Museum of Modern Art in New York for safekeeping.

Josep Lluís Sert. Pavilion of the Spanish Republic, International Exposition in Paris, 1937. In background, Pablo Picasso's *Guernica* (1937)

Following the devastation of World War II, Europe was rebuilt in a decidedly modern manner even as many of its masters remained abroad: Mies was teaching at the Illinois Institute of Technology in Chicago and Sert was living in different American cities before settling in Cambridge in 1953, replacing Walter Gropius—another European exile—as dean of Harvard's Graduate School of Design. By then, the Cold War had made Francisco Franco, the Spanish dictator who seized power during the country's civil war, a valuable anticommunist ally of the West. The isolation that followed the end of the war turned into reluctant acceptance, opening up a regime that after 1959 adopted a liberal, growth-oriented economy. Ironically, it was in the chill of the Cold War period that the wounds of previous conflicts began to heal. By the 1960s, both Sert and Mies were again building in their native lands, as were many of their fellow countrymen.

Modern architecture, banned in Spain for two decades for ideological reasons, returned to the country in the late 1950s. The style was fitting for the optimistic mood that accompanied newfound economic growth. During the years that followed, both old, politically conservative masters—José Antonio Coderch, Miguel Fisac, Alejandro de la Sota, Francisco Javier Sáenz de Oiza—and young, rebellious neophytes—Oriol Bohigas, Antonio Fernández Alba, Fernando Higueras, Antonio Vázquez de Castro—shared the idiom of modernity. Yet if economic and artistic freedoms were attained in the 1960s, political liberties would have to wait until democracy was reestablished in 1977—the year the Spanish Constitution was approved—under King Juan Carlos. When the ephemeral pavilions of Mies and Sert were rebuilt in Barcelona in the 1980s, their rebirth had both an aesthetic and a civic meaning.

The establishment of democratic institutions did not take place without unrest, and the uncertainties of change coincided with a period of economic depression following the ideological upheaval of the 1960s and the energy crises of 1973 and 1979. In the field of architecture, these changes were expressed in Spain and elsewhere by the neoliberal populism of Robert Venturi and the Marxist contextualism of Aldo Rossi, whose postmodern— or antimodern—reactions would gain the favor of the young. In Spain, this time of flux came to a close in 1981 with the failure of a military coup in February and, in an international show of support for political reforms, the symbolic return of *Guernica* from MoMA in September. This demonstration of faith in the fledgling democracy was vindicated the following year with the orderly change of government following the Socialist Party's electoral victory.

In the last quarter of the century, Spain has had moments of collective pride, including its entry into the European Union in 1986 and its hosting in 1992 of both the Olympics in Barcelona and the World's Fair in Sevilla, and periods of disillusionment, including the scandals that brought down the socialist government in 1996 and the Madrid train bombings in 2004. But its architecture has shown a persistent record of aesthetic achievement and material consistency, being both true to its roots and open to new influences, as illustrated by the careers of Ricardo Bofill in the 1980s, Rafael Moneo in the 1990s, and Santiago Calatrava today. Spanish architects have also made their mark abroad, one especially notable example being Enric Miralles's Scottish Parliament, which was completed after his untimely death.

Now, twenty-five years after *Guernica*'s return, The Museum of Modern Art brings to New York a fine selection of current Spanish architecture, following an extraordinary research effort that involved visiting more than fifty architects' offices and more than one hundred building sites in forty different cities. This survey includes works from throughout Spain by architects both young and old from all corners of the country. The growing presence of work by foreign architects in Spain is also reflected here, with projects that demonstrate a general willingness to take risks, innovate, and pursue excellence in architectural patronage. For Spain, the notion of modernity has become inseparable from the opening of its borders to the winds of change. Once secluded, now open, Spain looks for its reflection in the eyes of others and finds itself disclosed in their gaze.

LUIS FERNÁNDEZ-GALIANO

Contemporary Architecture in Spain: SHAKING OFF THE DUST

TERENCE RILEY

In eleventh-century Europe, following the uneventful passing of the feared first millennium, so much building was underway that a monk later recalled, "It was as if the whole world had shaken off the dust of the ages and covered itself in a white mantle of churches."[1] A millennium later, Spain is again shaking off "the dust of the ages," creating itself a mantle not of churches—of which it has plenty—but of airports, museums, hospitals, libraries, train stations, stadiums, and auditoriums. Virtually every region of the country boasts a wave of new works of architecture—recently completed or in construction—of the highest design ambition. In what might be considered the last, late burst of the Enlightenment, Spain seems determined to correct the civil and cultural deficits that are a legacy not only of General Francisco Franco's military rule from 1939 to 1975 but also of the Counter-Reformation's mix of authoritarianism and religious orthodoxy.

The sheer scale of its building program is less important than the number of new projects that have, in recent years, given Spain a reputation as an international stage for architectural innovation and experimentation. These projects range from the single-family house—the universal crucible for radical experimentation—to what was until recently the largest construction site in Europe, the new Barajas Airport Terminals in Madrid (pp. 38–39). The latter, designed by the London-based Richard Rogers Partnership and Estudio Lamela from Madrid, underscores another notable aspect of the current wave of architecture in Spain: it includes the work not only of Spanish architects but of dozens of acclaimed architects from around the world. Also notable is the age of those participating in this particular moment in Spain's architectural history. Not only do more-established architects have many opportunities to build in Spain but so do much younger professionals, a remarkable contrast to the situation of previous generations.

Enric Miralles and Carme Pinós. Igualada Cemetery Park, Igualada, Barcelona. 1985–94

Looking to recent history for clues to explain Spain's emergence as a laboratory for contemporary architecture, its hosting in 1992 of both the World's Fair in Sevilla and the 25th Olympiad in Barcelona was undoubtedly a catalyst. The previous year, the country had already taken a step toward the forefront of international architecture when the Basque government signed an agreement with the Solomon R. Guggenheim Museum in New York to finance and construct a museum in the aging industrial city of Bilbao. By the time of its completion six years later, to the acclaimed designs of Los Angeles architect Frank Gehry, Spain was also, like so many nations around the globe, self-consciously mapping its course for the next millennium through a number of ambitious architectural projects, such as the expansion and renovation of the venerable Museo del Prado by Rafael Moneo (fig. 1) and the vast City of Arts and Sciences in Valencia by locally born Santiago Calatrava (fig. 2).

FIG. 1. Rafael Moneo. Museo del Prado Expansion, Madrid. 1996–present. Transverse section showing new construction at center

FIG. 2. Santiago Calatrava. City of Arts and Sciences (with Planetarium in foreground and Opera House in background), Valencia. 1996–2006

These architectural milestones of the 1990s need not have foreordained Spain's post-2000 surge in architectural aspiration and accomplishment. Numerous countries that have hosted World's Fairs or Olympic Games have found themselves with little to show for it but public debt and outsized and underused facilities. And a good number of the "millennial" projects heralded just a few years ago now seem hopelessly misconceived and cast a critical shadow over the cities and regions where they were built. Inasmuch, the questions to be explored here are: Why Spain? Why now?

There is, of course, no single or simple answer to these questions. Those familiar with its recent history alone could easily be unaware of how far Spain has developed in a relatively short time. But before jumping to recent strides it is helpful to first consider issues fundamental to the country's earlier development. The change in Spain's geopolitical status between the sixteenth and seventeenth centuries, when it was the center of a global empire, and the eighteenth and nineteenth centuries, when it was eclipsed by its European rivals, reflects the shift from the age of conquest and discovery to that of mercantilism and industry. Spain was, for numerous reasons, uniquely prepared for the former and seemingly incapable of coming to terms with the latter. By the twentieth century, Spain was far behind England, France, and Germany politically and economically. When Franco seized power, he added yet another chapter to Spain's turbulent national politics in the first decades of the twentieth century: his regime was founded in a devastating civil war that overthrew an eight-year-old republic, which had been preceded by a previous military dictatorship and a Bourbon monarchy.

Spain's economy began to improve dramatically beginning around 1960, when per capita income was just over $300 per year, far behind other industrialized nations.[2] While the economy faltered during the transition to democratic rule after Franco's death in 1975, which coincided with the global oil crisis in the mid-1970s, per capita income had nevertheless risen to $1,500 per year.[3] From 1986, the year Spain joined the European Union, until 1990 the economy boomed, averaging five percent annual growth.[4] Since then the country has experienced stronger and weaker periods but can generally be characterized by stable and at times robust growth, with unrealized potential for further growth.[5] By 2004 Spain's per capita income had risen to more than $23,000 per year, just fourteen percent less than the EU as a whole, and its per capita gross domestic product is now ninety percent of that of the EU average.[6]

Three elements underpinned the economic growth in the latter years of the Franco regime. The first was the liberalization of Spain's finance laws, particularly those intended to attract foreign investment. The second was the flow of money into the country sent by the 1 million Spanish citizens (eight percent of the work force) working abroad.[7] The third pillar of this growth was the development of tourism as a national industry. Of the three, tourism undoubtedly had the greatest direct effect on the built environment of both Spain's cities and rural areas. In 1960, 4 million tourists from abroad visited Spain.[8] The subsequent rise in the economy over the next fifteen years was paralleled by an equally strong surge in tourism: by 1975, 32 million foreign tourists were arriving annually in Spain, making it the most important sector for economic growth.[9]

The expansion of the built environment followed suit as the country rushed to provide accommodation for both its quickly growing population and a near equal number of visitors. Moreover, Spain's population was not only increasing rapidly but migrating in large numbers from the countryside to the cities. The *éxodo rural* during the Franco years saw every region in Spain lose population except those with cities with the highest concentration of industry.[10] In and around Madrid, Barcelona, Bilbao, and Valencia, hundreds of thousands of housing units, the quality of which generally reflected a lack of coherent planning and an even greater lack of architectural sensitivity, were rapidly constructed. In the wake of the tourist boom, Spain's Mediterranean shores, which had supported a string of cities and towns from the Pyrenees to Gibraltar for over 2,500 years, became in places a continuous band of coastal development with every manner of tourist accommodation, little of which had any architectural merit.[11] The great majority of the buildings constructed for the tourist industry throughout Spain, as elsewhere, reflected more closely the needs and fantasies of the tourists that fleetingly inhabited them than any local or regional architectural culture. No doubt Franco would have preferred to think of the official monuments he decreed as his imprint on the nation. But the built landscape of Spain—twenty percent larger than the state of California—was far more altered by the explosive and unregulated growth of Spain's cities and the proliferation of tourist accommodations throughout every corner of the country during the latter part of his regime: on average, nine new hotels and hostels were opened *each week* for the last fifteen years of his rule.[12]

ALL ROADS LEAD TO EUROPE

If the tourist hotel could be considered a virtual hallmark of Franco-era economic success, it cannot be seen as emblematic of Spain's position today. In the last twenty years the country has undertaken the most extensive building and rebuilding of its civil infrastructure since the Romans unified the Iberian Peninsula with roadways and aqueducts during the reign of Augustus. In recent years, the Spanish construction industry has eclipsed tourism

FIG. 3. Cruz y Ortiz. Santa Justa Railway Station, Sevilla. 1987–91

FIG. 4. Santiago Calatrava. Alamillo Bridge, Sevilla. 1987–92

and led all the other basic economic sectors. Rather than conforming to tourists' expectations, the recent wave of construction in Spain—much of which has been devoted to civil works—reflects a new sense of self-definition.

The adoption of democratic institutions was a precondition for Spain joining the European Union in 1986. While that reform should be considered a national achievement of the highest order in and of itself, Spain also began to benefit immediately from one of the EU's objectives: to equalize the standard of living among its constituents. Poorer countries became net receivers while richer ones became net contributors of funds to achieve the goal of minimizing the differences in basic living conditions within the EU. Under programs meant to encourage infrastructure projects, Spain has received nearly $110 billion in funding over the last twenty years toward the construction of new highways, bridges, railroads, train stations, airports, and more, making it the largest net receiver of any EU member.[13] That there was a need for such projects might best be illustrated by the fact that until 1978 Spain's rail lines did not conform to European standards. Trains traveling from Europe could not operate on Spanish tracks and vice versa, meaning passengers were required to stop at the border not only for passport control but to change trains as well. Not simply a technical issue, this discrepancy reflected a governmental policy of self-isolation.

Beyond integrating its rail system with Europe, a high-speed train between Madrid and Sevilla was inaugurated at the time of the World's Fair and was the first in a planned network of nearly 4,500 miles of track that will ensure that future travel time from all of the provincial cities to the capital will be four hours or less.[14] In addition to a new train station designed by local architects Antonio Cruz and Antonio Ortiz (fig. 3), Sevilla also opened a new airport extension designed by Moneo and the lyrical Alamillo Bridge designed by Calatrava (fig. 4). The next major step in the construction of the high-speed rail network will be the new station in the Sagrera district of Barcelona, which, when begun, will be the largest construction site and the most ambitious development project in Spain, comprising 50 hectares devoted to not only the transport hub but also adjacent housing, offices, and retail development.

Other cities are also being transformed by the building and rebuilding of their transportation networks. In Bilbao, an airport and pedestrian bridge designed by Calatrava, another bridge by Lorenzo Fernández Ordóñez, and new subway stations by Foster and Partners were all completed in the last ten years. Madrid's 7.5-million-square-foot terminals for the Barajas Airport are conceived as international gateways between Europe and the Americas, though no less ambition can be seen in the designs for smaller airports such as the Canarian firm N.Tres's recently completed project in Tenerife (pp. 268–69).[15]

Just as the transformation of Spain's transportation infrastructure continues to unfold, so does the tourist industry that began to characterize the country's economic growth before 1975, and on which it still relies today.[16] Throughout the Franco years the tourist industry tried at various times to balance the lure of the low-cost beaches of the south with that of its historical cities inland. The restoration of monasteries and castles as *paradores*— a unique form of tourist accommodation—sets the tone for this campaign.

The recent wave of construction, however, signals a plan to further transform the nature of tourism in Spain, offering options other than sunny indolence and historical pageantry. The development of the concept of "cultural tourism" has been hugely affected not only by external changes—such as lower-cost vacation options now available in North Africa, the Caribbean, and elsewhere—but by internal ones as well, not least of all the success of the Guggenheim Bilbao (fig. 5) at attracting tourists from all over the world to see

FIG. 5. Gehry Partners. Guggenheim Museum, Bilbao. 1991–97

its architecture as much as its programs. Projects that correspond to a more contemporary idea of international tourism, such as Francisco Leiva Ivorra and grupo aranea's spa in Gijón (pp. 180–85), Rem Koolhaas and Ellen van Loon's Congress Center in Córdoba (pp. 192–97), and Gehry and Edwin Chan's new boutique hotel for the Marqués de Riscal Winery in Elciego (pp. 122–27), are all emblematic of a broad departure from the standard architectural product of the Spanish tourist industry in the 1960s and 1970s. In yet another demonstration of the changes in the national mood, even the "golden goose" of tourism is now subject to reinterpretation.

FIG. 6. RCR Arquitectes. Indoor Pool, Manlleu, Barcelona. 2001–present. Computer-generated image

In addition to civil infrastructure, Spain is also in the midst of a building boom to address its cultural and social infrastructure. A good portion of this activity can be found in and around the country's largest cities. However, the devolution of administrative power from Spain's central government to its seventeen regional governments has ensured that the phenomenon is widespread.[17] Today, the construction sites of the Arts Center in La Coruña by Victoria Acebo and Ángel Alonso (pp. 100–03), the Municipal Theater in Torrevieja by Foreign Office Architects (pp. 70–75), and the swimming hall near Barcelona by RCR Arquitectes (fig. 6) outline a network of activity that extends from the Atlantic coast to the Mediterranean to the Pyrenees. While the infrastructure projects previously discussed were largely paid for with EU funds, the cultural and social facilities being constructed by Spain's regional governments are largely paid for with tax money distributed by the central government. An expression of the political will, Spain's investment in its cultural and social infrastructure matches in spirit the EU's investment in its public works.

The establishment of the Museo Nacional Centro de Arte Reina Sofía in Madrid in 1986 and the Institut Valencià d'Art Modern (IVAM) in 1989 can be seen as examples of the desire not only to redefine Spanish culture in contemporary as well as historical terms but to further develop the country as a site for a new and more sophisticated kind of tourism. In their earliest years, the goal of these institutions might have been seen as simply catching up with other institutions in Europe and elsewhere. Their subsequent histories, however, demonstrate expanding reputations and programs matched by equally ambitious architecture. The Reina Sofía Museum, originally an eighteenth-century hospital, was first renovated to the designs of architects Antonio Fernández Alba, José Luis Iñiguez de Onzoño, and Antonio Vázquez de Castro. To handle the increasing number of visitors, glass elevators designed by Ian Ritchie were added on the exterior of the main facade in 1990, and a new wing designed by Jean Nouvel was completed last year (pp. 86–87). IVAM has enjoyed a similar rise both in stature and in the scale of its physical premises. Emilio Giménez and Carlos Salvadores designed the original structure. Giménez and Julián Esteban later carried out subsequent interior remodeling and Ryue Nishizawa and Kazuyo Sejima have designed a major addition (pp. 144–49). Reflecting the private sector's contributions, Spain's largest savings bank established the eponymous Fundació "La Caixa" in 1991 and embarked on a program to establish a series of new municipal galleries throughout the country devoted to exhibiting its corporate collections and other changing art exhibitions. In 2002 the CaixaForum in Barcelona, located in a nineteenth-century building designed by Josep Puig i Cadafalch and renovated and expanded by Arata Isozaki and Roberto Luna, inaugurated the program, and currently projects in Madrid (fig. 7) and La Coruña, designed by Herzog & de Meuron and Nicholas Grimshaw, respectively, are in construction. Along with Richard Meier's 1995 Museum of Contemporary Art in Barcelona and the Guggenheim Museum in Bilbao, these new initiatives—both in terms of their architecture and their programs—represent an eagerness to compete internationally as centers of cultural activity. But Spain's commitment to contemporary culture is evident in smaller cities as well. The Museum of Contemporary Art (MUSAC) in León (pp. 130–31), designed by Luis Mansilla and Emilio Tuñón, and the Oscar Domínguez Institute of Contemporary Art and Culture in Santa Cruz de Tenerife (fig. 8), designed by Herzog & de Meuron and now under construction, further serve as emblems of the national mood.

Another indication of that mood is the appearance of relatively tall buildings in many cities that have traditionally been characterized by low-rise construction. Recent skyscraper

FIG. 7. Herzog & de Meuron. CaixaForum, Madrid. 2001–06. Computer-generated image

FIG. 8. Herzog & de Meuron. Oscar Domínguez Institute of Contemporary Art and Culture, Santa Cruz de Tenerife. 1999–2007. Computer-generated image

projects by Jean Nouvel (pp. 224–25) and Enric Miralles and Benedetta Tagliabue (pp. 240–45) now have a notable sculptural presence on the skyline of Barcelona. Calatrava has also proposed three towers, similar to that which he recently completed in Malmö, Sweden, in the city of Valencia. Innovation and experimentation are also evident in smaller, mid-rise projects by younger architects. Vicente Guallart's Sharing Tower (pp. 150–55), under construction in Valencia, proposes radically different spatial configurations for a variety of low-income residents—providing less private space and more shared space—modeled on various forms of ad hoc communal life. Iñaki Ábalos, Juan Herreros, and Renata Sentkiewicz's Bioclimatic Towers (pp. 168–73) for Vitoria-Gastéiz explore energy efficiency at a level much higher than that mandated by law, employing solar panels as the exterior skin of the building and other measures.

The current building boom can then be seen as a timely intersection of a substantial need with substantial means. That said, Spain can't claim that economic growth has had a beneficial effect on new architecture across the board. For example, the often unintelligible suburban growth of the outlying areas of most of its major cities or the ever-expanding tourist areas in the south demonstrate that, like most other industrialized countries, Spain's best works of architecture are often incidental events within a larger sphere of building activity with much lower aspirations. Even so, the number of exceptional projects being built in Spain in recent years is unquestionably high.

It is impossible to quantify or even identify with certainty the conditions that produce good architecture or any other complex endeavor, in Spain or elsewhere. A number of factors, however, can be considered as having a positive influence in promoting the development of a strong contemporary architectural culture in Spain. Some of these factors are attributable to the integration of Spain's cultural policies with those of the rest of Europe. One example is the somewhat recent legislation that requires that any building project that receives public funds must be initiated with an architectural competition, as is the case in most of Europe.[18] In such a process, architects—either a select group or, in the event of an open competition, any qualified architect who chooses to participate—submit designs to a jury charged with selecting the best one. While the competition system is hardly perfect, it has distinct advantages over one whereby an architect is selected based on past work, references, or even political connections or celebrity rather than on his or her proposal for the project at hand. Despite its faults, the competition system remains a proven way for good ideas and, often, lesser-known architects to rise to the top. Of the many competitions held each year, one biannual series, staged by the organization Europan, is unique and quite admirable in that it specifically seeks to promote the emerging talents of architects under forty years of age. Governments and private developers throughout Europe submit proposed projects to the organization, which then stages competitions for the projects selected.[19] Young Spanish architects as well as Spanish governmental agencies and private developers have been active in the Europan program since its inception in 1989. The most important benefit of the program is that it gives younger architects extraordinary opportunities to compete for actual commissions among their peers, providing rare chances to those qualified to build at a younger age. Two of the most notable successes of the Europan program can be found in Spain: the SE-30 Social Housing in Sevilla by Fuensanta Nieto and Enrique Sobejano (pp. 128–29) and the soccer stadium in Barakaldo, outside Bilbao, by Eduardo Arroyo (pp. 36–37).

A sad fact of the later years of the Franco regime was the number of Spaniards, professionals as well as laborers, who were living abroad in order to find work. Since 1986, this trend has reversed and Spain has benefited from the expertise obtained by its erstwhile expatriates. Within the European Union, travel or living abroad is now elective, with obviously increased opportunities for international exchange. Many talented younger architects have taken advantage of the opportunity to work abroad, and the number of architecture students studying outside of Spain has also increased substantially since 1986.[20] Further, an EU-wide effort known as the Erasmus Program is now underway with the goal of equalizing Europe's university systems so that a degree given in one country will be recognized by all. Its eventual completion will undoubtedly cause an even greater increase in Spanish students obtaining an international dimension to their education.

Spanish professionals have also found that they can compete quite effectively within the European Union and elsewhere for architectural commissions as well as appointments to teaching positions. For example, Ortiz and Cruz of Sevilla are currently planning the renovation of one of the Netherlands' national icons, the Rijksmuseum, and Calatrava is designing the new transit hub for the World Trade Center site in New York City. In addition to maintaining a large international practice, Moneo was chairman of the architecture department at Harvard University from 1985 to 1990 while Josep Lluís Mateo of Barcelona is currently a professor at the equally prestigious Eidgenössische Technische Hochschule in Zurich in addition to working on commissions in Prague and Zurich.

The privileges earned by joining the European Union are, of course, reciprocal, and the number of architects from Europe as well as Asia, North America, and South America working and teaching in Spain has also visibly increased. While some have expressed dismay at the number of commissions being awarded to architects from abroad, this reality needs to be seen in perspective. The increase in the number of foreign architects working in Spain might be a departure from recent practice, but it is not new within the country's larger architectural history. Many important monuments of both the Christian north and the Moorish south were designed and built by people from beyond the peninsula. The cathedrals of the pilgrimage route that extended from the Pyrenees to Santiago de Compostela were constructed by French, German, and Flemish builders and artisans. In the south, early monuments such as the Medinah al Zaharah palace complex outside of Córdoba are heavily indebted to the architects and craftsmen of the Umayyad dynasty, based in Damascus.[21]

Professional pride aside, it is also hard to deny the importance of the exchange that takes place when qualified architects engage in work in another country. For example, the mixed-use project designed by Álvaro Siza (pp. 54–59), from Portugal, is a masterful work

FIG. 9. Francisco Cabrero. Trade Union Building, Madrid. Watercolor on paper, 39 ⅜ x 27 ⁹/₁₆" (100 x 70 cm). 1949

that, like much of Siza's oeuvre, has a real resonance with the architectural traditions of the peninsula. Equally, when American Thom Mayne, the 2005 Pritzker Prize winner, brings his considerable talent to the issue of state-sponsored housing (pp. 262–67)—a building type whose strict limitations often discourage architects with other options—the profession as well as the occupants benefit.

SPAIN'S INDISSOLUBLE DIVERSITY

The risk that Spain might become the locus of some indistinguishable "Euro-architecture" is more than counterbalanced by a number of factors that, despite integration of much of the continent, favor a distinctive architecture or, more accurately, various distinctive modes of architectural expression across the country. The liveliness of the current wave of diverse architectural developments has a basis—no doubt unintended—in the country's Constitution of 1978, which emphasizes "the indissoluble unity of the Spanish Nation" but also tempers that unity with guarantees of autonomy to its constituent peoples and regions; in addition, the document recognizes the individual's "inviolable and inherent" right "to freely express and disseminate thoughts, ideas and opinions by word, in writing or by any other means." [22]

The best of Spanish architecture under Franco's rule, such as Francisco Cabrero and Rafael de Aburto's Trade Union Building in Madrid (fig. 9), was more vibrant than is often remembered. However, the regime's most emblematic project, the 1959 Valley of the Fallen near San Lorenzo de El Escorial (fig. 10), designed by Pedro Muguruza with, it is said, the participation of Franco himself,[23] is stark evidence of the stifling effect that authoritarian rule can have on innovation.[24] Autocratic states are not necessarily infertile ground for good architecture—the masterful works produced by Karl Friedrich Schinkel for King Frederick William IV of Prussia come to mind—but the Franco government's goal of promoting an official version of national identity over all else left little if any room for invention. Most of the monuments built throughout Spain under his rule employed a stripped-down classical style

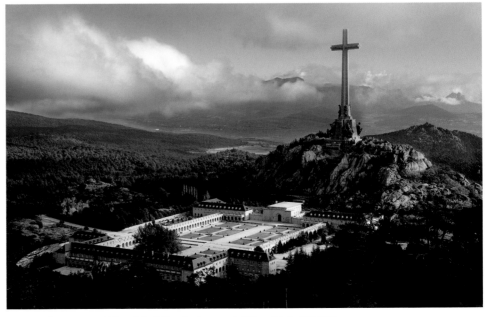

FIG. 10. Pedro Muguruza. Valley of the Fallen, San Lorenzo de El Escorial, Madrid. 1959

with symmetrical plans, massive stonework, and hierarchical composition. Recalling a popular description of architecture as "the alphabet of kings," the regime monopolized the design of public spaces and buildings for its own goals and through it communicated its core values: order, unity, permanence, and discipline.

Taking architecture as an alphabet—a system by which thought is expressed—the relevant questions with regard to contemporary architecture in Spain are: Whose expression? Expression of what? If there is a single underlying thread in recent architecture, it is its emergence as a potent critique of the kind of messages upon which Franco's nation-building rhetoric was dependent. In its willingness to recognize subjective perception and experience over universal narratives and its use of, among other techniques, complex geometries that are intended to accommodate rather than regulate daily life, contemporary architecture has incorporated "diversity" and "multiculturalism" not just as stylish labels but as part and parcel of its discourse.

The Canary Islands present a good example of the changes in architectural culture that can be seen through the prism of Spain's political transformation. Recognizing the strategic importance of this far-flung outpost, 828 miles south of the mainland and on the same latitude as the former colony of Spanish Sahara, Franco favored the islands with various civic projects, including the town hall and monument that still dominate the former commercial harbor of Santa Cruz de Tenerife (fig. 11). The stone tower of the overscaled 1943 town hall, designed by José Enrique Marrero Regalado in a pastiche of classical motifs, looms over the plaza and its monument, designed by Tomás Machado. The monument is a piece of true nationalist kitsch, a basalt cross dedicated to the unknown Francoist soldiers who died in the country's civil war, with split members that reveal glowing lights within.

In stark contrast to these derivative works are recent projects by architects who make serious efforts to address the unique cultural and physical landscape of this island environment. A partially open-air performing arts school by Juan Antonio González and Urbano Yanes Tuña of Tenerife (pp. 222–23) casts the city and the Atlantic Ocean beyond as its backdrop, while taking full advantage of the island's climate. The airport designed by N.Tres, previously mentioned, goes against the grain of current airport design and, like the theater school, incorporates the landscape, framing the mountain range that parallels its runways. A stadium designed by Felipe Artengo Rufino, Fernando Martín Menis, and José M. Rodríguez-Pastrana Malagón (pp. 134–39), also Canarians, is being constructed of local stone and appears to be a monumental earthwork.[25] On the nearby island of Gran Canaria, the high-rise Woermann Complex by Abalos&Herreros with CASARIEGO/GUERRA, arquitectos (pp. 82–83) incorporates panels that reflect the local fauna and geology and two museums in historic structures have been designed by Nieto and Sobejano to showcase the islands' culture.

The regional architectural expression found in the Canaries and throughout the country show Spain to be what historian John Crow might have called an *authentically* diverse environment, able and willing to support contemporary cultural aspirations: "Spain is heterogeneous at the base and heterodoxy is her religion. The only common denominator is that of sharing the same land and same history which has created Spaniards out of something that was not Spanish before."[26] Crow's characterization explains not only why Franco's attempts to create a single mode of Spanish national expression were so banal but also why the current wave of architecture is so diverse in its modes of expression and why it is so convincingly so.

FIG. 11. José Enrique Marrero Regalado. Town Hall (1943, back left); Tomás Machado. Monument to the Fallen (1944, foreground), Santa Cruz de Tenerife

If, under Franco, architecture was reserved as the alphabet of kings, Catalan architect Enric Miralles, working with Carme Pinós and later Benedetta Tagliabue, more than any other legitimized the full potential for architecture to be an alphabet of individuals. While fully participating in what has been called the lyrical architectural mode of Catalunya, Miralles's work subordinated those influences to a powerfully synthetic imagination that produced extraordinary results of great personal expression. The Igualada Cemetery Park (1985–94; see p. 10), designed with Pinós, is an excellent example of his ability to redefine an architectural type, in this case one laden with centuries of precedent, in a language that is not only expressive but poetic.

In recent years building projects throughout Spain have become accepted—albeit not without some contestation—as opportunities for architects to experiment with space and form, in some instances with surprisingly few restraints. The crisp origami-like chapel designed by Sol Madridejos and Juan Carlos Sancho Osinaga and built near Ciudad Real (pp. 40–41) and Peter Eisenman's vast sculpted landscape of the City of Culture of Galicia (pp. 48–53), now under construction in Santiago de Compostela, are two excellent examples among many. Some may see the emergence of architecture as a powerful form of personal expression as a momentary swinging of the pendulum, but this point of view is overly colored by the memory of Franco's long rule. His years of authoritarianism have tended to under-score the moments in history when Spain, for various reasons, succumbed to political abso-lutism and religious orthodoxy. But those years and the memories of them have also obscured the country's long and deeply held ideal of the self-realized individual as the true expression of Spanish culture, whether seen in the fictional character Don Quixote or actual artists such as his author, Miguel de Cervantes, painter Diego Velázquez, or architect Antoni Gaudí. In this sense, the genuinely new element in Spain's recent embrace of architecture as a means of individual expression is not the expression itself but the relative emphasis on architecture as a medium.

Even so, the opportunity for self-expression through architecture is counterbalanced by a 1999 law, titled Ley de Ordenación de la Edificación, that assigns full legal responsibility to the architect from the design stage through construction. This represents a shift from recognizing a distinction between design architects, who conceive the building, and produc-tion architects, who prepare the detailed construction documents and supervise the work, as is increasingly the case elsewhere. While the basis of the law is no doubt to ensure an orderly building process and to protect the client and the public's interest, it is also particu-larly welcome to those who think that how a building is built is as important as what it looks like. Indeed, the lowest level of architectural accomplishment is often accompanied by an inverse increase in the number of architects specializing in one aspect of a project—design architects, production architects, interior architects, curtain wall architects, landscape archi-tects, and so on. The Taylorization of the design process may lead to increased efficiency in its various tasks but it equally dilutes the possibility of a unified vision of the project in the hands of a single author. Toyo Ito's organic, cocoonlike spa pavilions for a park in Torrevieja (pp. 88–93), for example, are nothing if not lyrical, but it is impossible to separate their appearance—both interior and exterior—from the manner in which they are being built; their forms are completely integral to how they are constructed.

The current wave of innovative architecture in Spain is not attributable solely to the architects involved or the laws that govern their practice but also to the regional and municipal leaders with the vision to support the projects. Such leaders, however, particularly those in charge of historical cities and regions, have rarely been associated in Spain or elsewhere with the sort of bold patronage that often enlivens metropolitan centers. Particularly in areas dependent on tourism, the default position of most decision-makers has been conservative with regard to changes in the physical environment. The so-called Bilbao effect describes the global impact that the construction of the Guggenheim Museum in that city has had not only on architecture but on a whole range of issues, including contemporary culture, politics, and finance.[27] However, the local dimension of the Bilbao effect might be seen as giving leaders an incentive to take chances with regard to architecture and urbanism, evident not only in the metropolitan areas but, notably, in smaller cities and towns across Spain as well.

An excellent case in point are the La Granja Escalators (pp. 272–73) designed by Élias Torres Tur and José Antonio Martínez Lapeña for Toledo, a walled medieval city justifiably proud of its architectural heritage that is now a regional governmental center as well as an important tourist destination. The purpose of the project—which consists of escalators, walkways, and overhead canopies that project from and are carved into the city's walls— was to create a way to move more easily and quickly from an underground parking lot at the base of the city's iconic fortified ramparts to the historic upper city. If not for an environment that encouraged risk-taking, it is nearly unthinkable that the city would have agreed to such a striking sculptural presence.

Similarly, León, a medieval cathedral city that was once the capital of the kingdom of Castilla y León, has built a number of important and innovative new structures that have recast the experience of residents and visitors alike. An impressive concert hall by Mansilla and Tuñón (who also designed the city's Museum of Contemporary Art) and Jordi Badia and Josep Val's starkly beautiful building for funerary preparations and services (fig. 12) have been constructed in the last six years.

FIG. 12. BAAS Jordi Badia and Josep Val. Mortuary, León. 1997–2001

URBAN RIGHTS, URBAN PRIVILEGES

These and other projects serve as reminders that Spain is by no means a blank slate. Its history of urban culture provides a unique frame of reference for distinctive contemporary architecture, the best of which recognizes and reacts to this complex and multilayered narrative. As real estate development has perfected itself internationally as a systematic way to commodify the built environment, the cost in many instances has been a stultifying homogenization of architecture. Perhaps no policy or program can be imagined that is more resistant to this homogenization—and more disposed to authentic local culture—than historic cities, of which Spain has many.

Spain's urban culture cannot be completely appreciated without some reference to these historic centers. Like much of Europe, Spain's most lasting urban roots lay in the Romanization of its preexisting cultures. As the Roman armies vanquished in 19 BC the last of the tribes that had inhabited the Iberian Peninsula, they implemented policies that were designed to make their new provinces more governable and to transplant Latin culture in the process. Reflecting the mix of destruction and construction that was the hallmark of their military strategy, the six Roman Legions that conquered what they called Hispania were also responsible for building the civil works that would unify it.

As an inducement for both Roman settlers and native-dwellers to gravitate toward the key urban centers of Hispania, special rights and privileges were granted to the inhabitants of the newly created colonial towns as well as strategic existing towns and cities that had been designated *municipia*. Under Augustus's rule, one hundred sizable colonial towns, *municipia*, and smaller townships—close to one-fourth of the peninsula's total—were granted such rights and privileges.[28] As the Romans built up urban centers they also connected them, building over 12,000 miles of highways.[29] Most notable is the Via Augusta, constructed in just three years, which began at the Pyrenees and ran nearly 1,000 miles southwest to Cádiz, not far from the Strait of Gibraltar.[30]

The Romans' policies of urbanization have an echo in those set forth by the Christian kings during the Reconquest, the eight-century struggle to expel the Moors that had invaded Spain from North Africa in the eighth century. Recalling the strategic designation of *municipia*, the Christian kings also granted special privileges—*fueros*—to induce the recolonization of the often dangerous and ever-shifting frontier between the Christian north and Moorish south.[31] Defensive in nature, the towns and villages of what became the Spanish heartland were and remain more urban, despite their smaller size, than those in the typical agricultural landscape elsewhere in Europe. In the words of the philosopher Miguel de Unamuno:

> The population of the Castilian country-side is concentrated for the most part in hamlets, villages or towns, in groups of clustered dwelling houses, separated from one another by immense and naked solitudes. The villages are compact and sharply delineated, not melting away into the plain in a surrounding fringe of isolated homesteads, the intervening country being entirely unpopulated.[32]

The successive policies of encouraging urban dwelling have left a mark on Spain that is nothing short of remarkable. Of the one hundred sizable towns and townships on the peninsula cultivated by the Romans, seventy are still inhabited, ranging in size from villages such as Tiermes, which lies 100 miles north of Madrid and has a population of 250 (originally a mid-size town known as Termantia), to Barcelona, with a metropolitan population of 3.9 million inhabitants (then known as Barcino and only half the size of Termantia). In total, the urbanization programs initiated by the Romans over two thousand years ago support a population of approximately 11.5 million people today, more than a quarter of Spain's current population.[33]

It is not difficult to argue that the quality of contemporary architecture in Spain today is related to the strength of its urban character. The proximity of buildings in cities large and small provides the same sort of enriching dialogue that is experienced with works of art in a museum. While some may find urban conditions to be restraining, it is that very restraint that often gives rise to unique and meaningful solutions. The Town Hall Extension for the city of Murcia (pp. 178–79) designed by Moneo and completed in 1998 is an excellent case in point. Situated on the narrow end of an urban square dominated by a baroque cathedral, Moneo created a screen facade with asymmetrically balanced openings that enlivens his building's appearance in relation to the ornate cathedral opposite it. The porosity of the facade also adds a palpable depth to the building, which otherwise could have appeared two-dimensional, its actual volume being obscured by the narrowing of the plaza. These design decisions have no idealized value in and of themselves but are derived from the unique situation of the building's dense urban condition.

Of course in Roman times, density would have been valued for the security it afforded and the commerce it sustained. Culture and the sense of what we recognize as the public realm would not have been so evident at the outset. As noted by historian Josh Cook, the growth of urban life led to, among other things, a rise in literacy and the adoption of the Latin language, which became a conduit for the proliferation of Roman civic values in Spain. Local elites, who were groomed by the Romans, thus became, like their counterparts elsewhere in the empire, responsible for the adoption of Roman cultural policies, especially the construction of public spaces and buildings.[34]

In this respect, the Moors had much more in common with the Romans than the various northern tribes (and their pious Christian descendants) that had wrested control of Hispania from the late Roman Empire three hundred years earlier. Unsurprisingly, Moorish culture in Spain—not least of all its architecture—flourished in urban centers, most spectacularly in Córdoba, Sevilla, and Granada. While different sources provide vastly different statistics, Córdoba is largely recognized as having been "the largest, the wealthiest, and the most civilized city in western Europe in the tenth century."[35]

Over time the benefits of such cities as the Romans and the Moors created were not only appreciated by their inhabitants but came to be expected. These same high expectations are evident in the current efforts across Spain to expand and refine the country's inventory of public buildings devoted not only to infrastructure and culture, as we have seen, but to other aspects of urban life that might be considered part of a "civilized" city, such as housing, social services, medicine, and sports. The neighborhood social services center designed by Carlos Ferrater and Lucia Ferrater and constructed in Barcelona (pp. 84–85) and the health center designed by Mario Corea and Lluís Morán for Santa Eulalia on the island of Ibiza (pp. 132–33) are emblematic of how many of Spain's cities respond to these aspirations. Rather than centralize the mandated social, educational, and medical services in larger but more distant structures, all of them are provided, in the case of Barcelona, within each of the city's forty-one traditional barrios, stabilizing and enlivening the neighborhoods as well as providing a rich urban architectural fabric. This sensitivity to urban life can also be seen in the scale of the previously described athletic facilities—the 8,000-seat stadium in Barakaldo or the 10,000-seat stadium now being built in Santa Cruz de Tenerife. While each may be less efficient economically than larger, more centralized facilities, their scale is also less destabilizing to the urban landscape than larger stadiums that draw in huge numbers of people for relatively short periods of time but remain for the most part large, mute presences in the neighborhoods they occupy.

By far, however, the most important building block of urban life is housing, and Spain remains committed to supporting the construction of housing in many forms. MVRDV's Edificio Mirador housing project outside Madrid (pp. 270–71) is no doubt one of the most adventurous examples of the more than 500,000 housing units built in Spain in 2003, nine percent of which were reserved for low-income renters.[36] Midway up the facade of the building, which was designed by the Dutch firm in collaboration with Blanca Lleó, a five-story open space serves as a public plaza for the neighborhood as well as a place to view the surroundings, or *mirador*. In order to address current and future needs, Spain will have to continue to build residential units on this scale for many years to come. Despite the tight budgets and restrictive requirements inherent to housing projects, the number of younger architects applying new thinking to their design would indicate that housing will continue to be a source of architectural and urban invention.

The dialogue between buildings within a dense urban fabric can also coalesce into a broader discourse that is sustained over time, as is evident in the very different architectural cultures of Madrid, founded as the seat of an austere and pious monarchy in the central highlands, and Barcelona, an independent-minded hub of mercantile and arts activity on the Mediterranean Sea. As has been noted by Spanish critic and publisher Luis Fernández-Galiano, "The line between Madrid pragmatism and Catalan lyricism is no mere cliché."[37]

The lyricism of Catalan architecture is rooted in the city's emergence as an industrial and commercial center in the mid-nineteenth century. The expressive and fantastic architectural language of art nouveau—an often enigmatic hallmark of the age—is interpreted most singularly in Catalunya by Antoni Gaudí, whose works can be seen throughout the city. A sense of the past continues to influence contemporary work in Barcelona. The recently completed Santa Caterina Market (pp. 174–75), designed by Miralles and Tagliabue, is a spectacular example. Its undulating wave of a roof reinterprets the expressive manner prevalent in the city, and its riotously colored tiles reflect the polychrome art nouveau facades of the merchants' mansions and the public buildings those merchants sponsored.

No less freely conceived is Enric Ruiz-Geli's Hotel Habitat in Barcelona (pp. 104–09), the most notable feature of which is the mesh that wraps the habitable portion of the structure, as if cosseting it within a spider web. At the interstices of the mesh, five thousand devices combining photovoltaic cells and LEDs absorb light during the day and cast it off at night, giving the building an ethereal presence. Conceived with artist Vito Acconci and architect Ruy Ohtake, the hotel pushes the boundary between art, architecture, and performance.

Any architecture can be said to be prosaic in comparison to the colorful surfaces and sinuously organic forms of the works of Gaudí, but the architecture of Madrid might be seen as having singularly pragmatic roots in its founding as the royal capital. Passing over more historic and noble cities, in 1561 Felipe II chose the then small and undistinguished Madrid as the capital principally for its central location.[38] (The efficacy of Felipe II's calculated decision is echoed today in the viability of the plans, previously discussed, to link all of the regions of Spain to the capital in under four hours.) The same pragmatic ethos can be seen in the contemporary work of Ábalos and Herreros, former students of Alejandro de la Sota and Francisco Javier Sáenz de Oiza, with whom they developed their interest in American architectural technology, in particular skyscrapers. Their emphasis on technological innovation, unbound by local or national traditions, as a means to solve architectural problems is an essentially pragmatic attitude and is evident not only in their designs for tall buildings but in their research on energy efficiency and environmental design as well.

Yet Ábalos and Herreros are hardly typical of Madrid's architectural scene, which is far more indebted to the leadership of Rafael Moneo as a practitioner, writer, and teacher. Since the construction of his National Museum of Roman Art in Mérida (fig. 13), Moneo and the architects who studied and worked under him have been rightly characterized as particularly sensitive to local architectural traditions and historic context, which might beg the question: How might that also be considered pragmatic?

FIG. 13. Rafael Moneo. National Museum of Roman Art, Mérida. 1980–85

FIG. 14. Juan Bautista de Toledo and Juan de Herrera. Royal monastery, San Lorenzo de El Escorial, Madrid. 1563–84

If one considers architecture to be the solution to a problem, the result will necessarily depend on the nature of the problem posed. In Le Corbusier's 1922–25 Plan Voisin for Paris, the solution, which called for the razing of almost 400 hectares of the city center, totally disregarded the historic urban fabric as one of the "facts" of the problem, focusing instead on traffic, light, construction, etc. In Moneo's design for the extension to the Museo del Prado, currently under construction, a very different approach is taken where, among all other considerations, the facts of the building, its site, and its history are melded into the larger description of the architectural problem. Hardly historicist, Moneo's work suggests that history is a process rather than an immutable past. If his work can be seen as reserved or cool that, too, has historical precedent. Felipe II's preference for a rather severe interpretation of Renaissance architecture, most evident in the royal monastery he commissioned at San Lorenzo de El Escorial (fig. 14), near Madrid, suggests less interest in aesthetic expressivity and more interest in classical order and historical models.

Yet looking around the country it is clear that in recent years the line between lyricism and pragmatism doesn't run just between Madrid and Barcelona. While most Barcelona architects still practice largely in Catalunya, if only for reasons of language, the number of innovative new projects around the country that have been authored by architects from Madrid is noteworthy. Still, the dialogue between the two appears to be robust enough to sustain itself and, moreover, healthy enough that neither side falls into parodies of themselves.

For example, the architects of Catalunya may be by reputation more emotionally expressive in their designs, but they are hardly dreamers whose works remain in the realm of fantasy. Like their colleagues elsewhere, they constitute a culture of builders. Furthermore, Barcelona is by far the most successful city in Spain in the often rough-and-tumble mix of architecture, politics, and public and private interests that is city planning. Ildefons Cerdà's well-maintained 1859 grid plan for the city's extension, with its slashing east–west diagonal boulevard has, like Manhattan's grid with its boogie-woogie-ing Broadway, been the highly rational launching pad from which so many of the city's architectural wonders have sprung.

Likewise, a number of architects associated with the more pragmatic side of the dialogue have recently demonstrated a willingness to expand beyond the formal boundaries

FIG. 15. Francisco Javier Sáenz de Oiza. Torre del BBVA, Madrid. 1972

FIG. 16. Francisco Mangado. Swimming Center, Leioa, Vizcaya. 2003

that characterize their earlier work and that of their mentors. The recent projects of architects Francisco Mangado, Mansilla, and Tuñón, all of whom studied with Moneo, and Ábalos and Herreros, for example, demonstrate a growing interest in more expressive geometries than one might associate with a pragmatist sensibility. Abalos & Herreros's Woermann Complex (pp. 82–83) is a sophisticated mix of visual cues that reflects market forces and technology as well as decidedly less objective references. The floor plans are rationally laid out to maximize usefulness and salability, and high-rise construction, of course, maximizes the developer's investment. The serrated profile, created by metal sunscreens projected at regular intervals, recalls that of the Torre del BBVA in Madrid (fig. 15), designed by Sáenz de Oiza, except that the upper floors of the complex's tower appear to be, delightfully if inexplicably, windblown by the prevailing breezes.

The plan of Mansilla and Tuñón's new Museum of Cantabria (pp. 42–47) has an irregular form overall but is composed of a single polygonal unit repeated throughout. The points at which the polygons meet create a grid of the same geometry, which serves as a planning device to create interior spaces and locate partitions and points of structure in a logical manner. In the vertical direction, however, the lines of the building ascend in an array of irregular profiles, recalling the region's mountainous landscape. Closer study of the crystalline forms reveals a systematic use of triangulated planes of various dimensions extending upward from the modular plan. While the underlying geometric logic is a suitably rational mechanism for creating architectural form, to the casual visitor the effect would be clearly and convincingly sculptural.

Mangado, too, has demonstrated a willingness to see where formal invention may take his architecture. In recent projects, such as the congress and exhibition center he is building in Ávila (pp. 234–39) and his swimming center in Leioa just outside Bilbao (fig. 16), the complexities of acoustics, topography, and waves are more fully expressed in a manner that is equally powerful, if not more so, than the simplicity of the cubic structures for which he is better known.

For these designers and any others who consider architecture the solution to a series of proposed problems, the "problem" of beauty is rarely discussed, if only for its resistance to analysis. For them, beauty is never an overtly expressed goal but something that might be discussed in hindsight, the consequence of a well-solved problem. Still, it seems less than accurate to think that the projects mentioned here and the great number of other frankly beautiful buildings constructed across Spain in the last few years are the unanticipated byproducts of diligent problem-solving alone. While their architects might describe their works in terms of algorithms, weather, topography, and more, the aura of geometers can also be considered a cover for what has been called "secret agents for beauty," a role quite rightly associated with the poet and essayist Tristan Tzara: "I have a mad and starry desire to assassinate beauty—the old kind, of course."[39]

THE EUROPEAN (AND MODERN) UNION

Spain's political and cultural renewal has happily coincided with a moment in contemporary architecture that theorist Anthony Vidler described thusly: "Following a decade of historical and typological exploration of 'false walls' and fake stones, postmodernism, the argument

FIG. 17. Ludwig Mies van der Rohe. Barcelona Pavilion, Barcelona. 1929

FIG. 18. Ludwig Mies van der Rohe. Barcelona Pavilion Reconstruction, Barcelona. 1986

goes, has been seen for what it was—the Potemkin City of the present—to be purified only by a renewed adhesion to the spirit of the age."[40] Even so, a reinvigorated commitment to the zeitgeist in terms of contemporary architecture in Spain necessarily carries a unique historical dimension that needs to be further considered.

Spain's experience of cultural and architectural renewal is certainly influenced by many events in its history, but it is also colored by what that history did not include: a full participation in the trajectory of modern architecture from its heroic initial stages in the 1920s through the various manifestations of postmodernism in the 1980s. A uniquely appropriate symbol of this absence is Ludwig Mies van der Rohe's masterful Barcelona Pavilion—built for and then dismantled after the 1929 International Exposition in Barcelona and rebuilt there in 1986 (figs. 17 and 18)—the seminal work of modern architecture in Spain that for fifty-seven years was *not* there.

Architectural historian Henry-Russell Hitchcock identified 1922 as the epiphanic moment for the wave of radical new architecture—known in German as the *Neues Bauen*—that was being built across Europe and beyond.[41] Its protagonists, Mies of Germany, Le Corbusier of France, and J. J. P. Oud of the Netherlands, along with a host of others, would in 1927 celebrate the first coalescence of the movement in the Weissenhof housing colony in Stuttgart. Consisting of twenty-one separate housing blocks—virtually all of them white, cubic structures designed by architects from four European countries—the colony was deemed emblematic of the new direction of architecture that would sweep away traditional national styles and incubate a new way of life for the twentieth century.

The *Neues Bauen*'s mix of architecture and social reform found tentative roots in Spain in the minds of those who supported both modernization—politically and otherwise—and closer ties with the rest of Europe. Emblematic in this regard was the young Catalan architect Josep Lluís Sert, who apprenticed in Le Corbusier's office in Paris in 1927. The tuberculosis clinic in Barcelona that he designed with Joan Baptista Subirana and Josep Torres-Clavé (fig. 19) was completed just before civil war broke out and remains a testament to Le Corbusier's influence as well as an expression of technological progress and the idea of architecture as an agent of social change. After Franco seized power in 1939, Sert, as did countless like-minded Spaniards, drew the logical conclusions and left for the United States and elsewhere.

While recognizing that there were and are many forms of modernism, it is the trajectory of this central movement, later known as the International Style, that has most come to represent the ideological course of modern architecture in the twentieth century. As with other such manifestations, its radical beginnings were mirrored in its equally banal ending, having become by the end of the 1960s little more than an official style of the Cold War and a symbol of corporate culture. The denouement of the International Style—which was celebrated in the 1980 exhibition *The Presence of the Past*, organized by Paolo Portoghesi—assumed not only a critique of its current status but the total discrediting of the ideology of its radical roots.[42] The two principal tools in this process were the return to historical models of architecture and the adaptation of the theories of subjectivity and relativism most often identified with the French philosopher Jacques Derrida, jointly considered manifestations of a post-modern culture.

The rebuilding of the Barcelona Pavilion coincided not only with the centenary of Mies's birth and the year of Spain's entry into the EU but with a moment when the novelty of post-modernism was waning. While there is no question that the latter day depredations of the then forty-year-old International Style deserved nothing but contempt, by 1986 the postmodern critique had occupied architectural theorists of one stripe or another for nearly half the time that the movement had proliferated around the world. One route out of the circular debates between modern and postmodern was the reinvestigation of modernism's constituent parts—International Style as well as other currents—in the search for that which has continued meaning today. Chief among the protagonists of this effort was the Dutch architect Rem Koolhaas, whose fascination with the reapparition of the pavilion and its architect is enshrined in a fictionalized history of the structure (fig. 20).[43] Koolhaas's essay-cum-fable describes the course of modern architecture before and after World War II and underscores Koolhaas's simultaneous rejection and embrace of that history and its protagonists.

No work other than the Barcelona Pavilion could symbolize the still fresh possibilities of a modern language of architecture. To the extent that modernism's supposed "coldness" had become a postmodern cliché, Mies's sensuous materials—red silk curtains, four different types of plate glass, and stone surfaces of golden onyx, Roman travertine, and green Alpine marble—fairly startled the eyes of those who had only known the structure from black-and-white photographs. Equally in keeping with the mood of the day were the spatial ambiguities and the palpable juxtapositions of the human figure—both the female nude of Georg Kolbe's statue *The Dawn* and the visitor's—with myriad abstract reflective surfaces. Given the particular vibrancy of that part of contemporary architecture in Spain that is directly or indirectly influenced by Mies's classic Minimalism—with newfound associations of material and spatial sensuousnes—it is hard to deny the importance of the Barcelona Pavilion's somewhat ahistorical reappearance. As if having arrived directly from the more radical moment of its creation, it exists as a negation of the International Style's subsequent dilutions and presents itself as a fresh point of departure.

While in any number of countries this same language of architecture enjoys a fashionable if somewhat emasculated revival, recent works by various architects working in Spain offer none of the cautionary apologetics that accompany the shelter magazines' promotion

FIG. 19. Josep Lluís Sert, Joan Baptista Subirana, and Josep Torres-Clavé. Tuberculosis Clinic, Barcelona. 1935

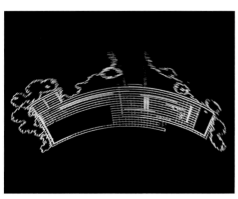

FIG. 20. Rem Koolhaas and Office for Metropolitan Architecture (OMA). "Bent" Barcelona Pavilion. Drawing. 1985

FIG. 21. RCR Arquitectes. Kindergarten, Manlleu, Barcelona. 2002–04

of the now domesticated "midcentury modern style." While that "style" is characterized by a palpably timid decorativeness, the mechanized Access to the Paseo del Ovalo in Teruel (similar in program to the escalator project in Toledo) by David Chipperfield Architects and b720 Arquitectos (pp. 176–77) is characterized by extravagantly large surfaces of steel plate with no superfluous concessions to the picturesque. Rather, the project unsentimentally maintains the urban scale necessary to counterbalance in time and space the remnants of the equally extravagant surfaces of the city's historic walls.

This and other recent projects in Spain with a frankly modern position should not be seen as an homage to Mies or any other modern master but as an appropriation—undertaken more freely than elsewhere—of what is available in the historical storehouse of twentieth-century architecture. RCR Arquitectes' Casa Rural in Girona (pp. 228–33) and their nearby kindergarten in Manlleu (fig. 21) have roots in Miesian composition, Minimalist art, and other sources but each demonstrates very different attitudes. The house looks like nothing if not a Donald Judd sculpture installed in the landscape, though its darkly rendered materials and inky shadows are evidence of a sensibility quite different from any obvious sources. The kindergarten, on the other hand, with its profusion of differently colored glass, seems to reformat the newly discovered but comparatively restrained polychromatic character of the Barcelona Pavilion as an environment where color and space are mutually dependent.

In these projects and many others, the current generation of Spanish architects—particularly the younger members—appears to have shrugged off their checkered inheritance and reestablished a vibrant architectural dialogue with relative ease. This can be seen, in part, as reflecting Vidler's "renewed adhesion to the spirit of the day." While that renewal can certainly be seen elsewhere, the vibrancy of the architectural discourse in Spain today is also due to its being neither overshadowed by the successes nor burdened by the failures of the main course of modern architecture in the twentieth century.

In this context, it is interesting to again consider the words of Miguel de Unamuno, who elegantly, if prejudicially, portrayed two paths to the future that Spain faced in the early part of the twentieth century. A fierce defender of what he saw as the country's unique national character, he criticized the aspirations of those who saw Spain as needing to remake itself in the image of its Continental neighbors:

> The term *European* expresses a vague idea, very vague, excessively vague; but much vaguer is the idea that is expressed by the term *modern*. If we combine the two together it would seem that they ought to limit one another and result in something concrete, and that the expression *modern European* ought to be clearer than either of its two components terms; but perhaps it is vaguer still.[44]

Arguing for passion over rationalism and traditional wisdom over science, he inverts what was then the progressive point of view. As exemplars, he invokes St. Augustine and Tertullian, both figures from the moment in history where one could be African, Roman, *and* Christian, and offers them as alternative paradigms for a culture influenced by all three:

> The great African, the great ancient African! Here you have an expression, ancient African, which can be opposed to modern European, and which is at least of equal value. St. Augustine was African and he was of the ancient world; so was Tertullian. And why should we not say: "We must Africanize ourselves ancientwise," or "We must ancientize ourselves Africanwise?"[45]

If Unamuno's polemical positions are thought of as two items on a national referendum, it is clear that since Franco's death Spain has overwhelmingly opted to be European and modern over anything else. Spain's integration with Europe has provided a matrix of positive factors that has clearly influenced the direction of contemporary architecture as well as every other aspect of its culture. In looking to Europe as a model, Spain not only accepted the comparisons that indicated its deficiencies in terms of civil and cultural infrastructures but in so doing also engaged in a concerted effort to correct those deficiencies. The systematic funding provided by the European Union to address the disparities between the standard of living— including the built environment—in Spain and the rest of the continent has proved to be an impressive matching of means with an identifiable goal. In many ways, Spain has been the European Union's greatest success and vice versa.

If Unamuno's negative characterizations of Europe and modernity have proved to be a minority viewpoint with regard to contemporary Spain, thoughtful observers will at least credit him with realizing that the meanings of the terms "European" and "modern" are not necessarily self-evident or immutable, in architecture or otherwise. Given Spain's singular course throughout much of the history of modern Europe, if it is now both modern, in the broadest sense, and European, one must ask how are its Europeanness and its modernity different from elsewhere on the continent?

On the face of it, Spain's Europeanness would have to be considered distinct from that of, say, France, Germany, or the Netherlands if only because of the way in which each came to see themselves as European. In the early 1950s, the Cold War allies north of the Pyrenees began the slow process of political and economic integration that resulted in the European Economic Community in 1957, the forerunner of the European Union. For the younger generation in those countries today, European identity is ingrained. Spain's integration with the European Union, on the other hand, came only after intense debate that extended well into its modern history. The country's very act of choosing its course required a reflective, as opposed to what might elsewhere be characterized as a reflexive, attitude with regard to things European and modern, which is evident not only in contemporary architecture but in other forms of cultural expression as well.

Spain's Europeanness is also distinguished by the historical experience that for so many centuries seemed to divide it from its neighbors. After all, electing to bind its future to that of Europe did not require Spain's dismissal of its history. Inasmuch, Spain's definition of European is one that includes a particular blend of Mediterranean, Roman, Moorish, and Atlantic cultures, with evident though largely untapped implications for its contemporary architecture. At the same time, Spain's evolving sense of modernity is, as we have seen, *less* defined by historical circumstance than elsewhere, creating if not a blank slate then a more open-ended framework for the exploration of the critical issues that defined modern culture and remain essential to contemporary life, no less architecture.

While much of the cultural scene in contemporary Spain, including architecture, has been influenced by the post-Franco desire to become a "normal" country within modern Europe, it is interesting to consider what will happen when normalcy becomes the norm, if it isn't happening already. While purely speculative at this point, it would not be unusual to see architects and other artists begin to focus on the more distinctive elements of their Europeanness or modernity to find a singular rather than a "normal" identity within Europe. Whether or not this comes to pass, this course holds greater promise for continued innovation in contemporary architecture than the idea of a "Spanish" style of architecture, as Unamuno might have argued for.

Nonetheless, it must be remembered that architecture is not a referendum in which a single choice must be made to the exclusion of all others. It has unique capacities for assimilation, aggregation, and interpolation. These capacities are appropriately evident in the Spanish plateresque style of architecture, unique to its own history, which combines Moorish, Gothic, and Renaissance elements. To cite its ability to find inclusive rather than exclusive modes of expression is not to say that architecture is, by any means, an art of compromise. Like any other genuine cultural endeavor, architecture is a competition of ideas. Its quality is most often dependent on how deeply held an idea might be and how it is best expressed. Polemical jousting such as passion versus reason, lyrical versus pragmatic, and past versus future continuously replenish architecture, and this is certainly true in the current wave of architecture in Spain. Like a political debate or a sporting match, these are conflicts that require true adherents, adherents who invariably produce the best results when one side never really vanquishes the other.

Notes

1. Rodulfus Glaber, *The Five Books of the Histories and The Life of St. William*, ed. and trans. John France, Neithard Bulst, and Paul Reynolds (Oxford: Clarendon Press, 1989), pp. 114–17.
2. John A. Crow, *Spain: The Root and the Flower. An Interpretation of Spain and the Spanish People*, 3rd ed. (Berkeley and Los Angeles: University of California Press, 1985), p. 371.
3. Ibid.
4. *The World Factbook*, "Spain: Economy: Overview," http://www.cia.gov/cia/publications/factbook/geos/sp.html#Econ.
5. "Economic Output Versus Potential," *The Economist*, August 27–September 2, 2005, p. 84.
6. Renwick McLean, "Spain Hopes to Stir Passion for Europe," *International Herald Tribune*, February 1, 2005.
7. Crow, *The Root and the Flower*, pp. 396–97. In a sign of how far the economy has progressed this situation has reversed, with 3 million registered immigrants in Spain sending €3.5 billion ($4.35 billion) abroad in 2004. Juan Jesús Aznárez, "The Fight for Immigrants' Money," *El País* (English-language edition), September 27, 2005.
8. Crow, *The Root and the Flower*, p. 377.
9. Ibid., pp. 376–77.
10. See Roser Nicolau, "La población," in *Estadísticas Históricas de España* (Barcelona: Banco Exterior, 1989).
11. For a history of the early settlement along this stretch of coastline, see William C. Atkinson, *A History of Spain and Portugal* (Harmondsworth, Middlesex, UK: Penguin Books, 1960), pp. 17–20.
12. Instituto Nacional de Estadística, "Anuario Estadístico 1963" and "Anuario Estadístico 1980," http://www.ine.es. To access the 1963 table, go to the English-language version of the website and follow the path History/Statistical yearbook/Anuario 1963/Resultados nacionales/Enseñanza, manifestaciones culturales, deportes y turismo/Turismo/Alojamientos hoteleros y camping/Alojamientos hoteleros en 31 de diciembre de cada año; for the 1980 table, follow the path History/Statistical yearbook/Anuario 1980/Totales nacionales/Turismo y otros servicios/Turismo/Establecimientos hoteleros clasificados y acampamentos/Establecimientos hoteleros clasificados en 31 de diciembre de cada año.
13. For information on funding for infrastructure projects in Spain, see Renwick McLean, "Financial History Lessons for Europe's New Members," *New York Times*, July 26, 2005.
14. SPG Media, "AVE High-Speed Rail Network, Spain," http://www.railway-technology.com/projects/spain.
15. The firm N.Tres has since disbanded, with the principal architects Antonio Corona and Arsenio P. Amaral starting the firm Corona y P.Amaral and the architect Eustaquio Martínez becoming a sole practitioner.
16. According to figures from the Instituto Nacional de Estadística, http://www.ine.es, 52.5 million people visited Spain in 2003. To access this information, go to the English-language version of the website and follow the path Services/Hotel industry and tourism/Tourism from abroad/Visitor entries broken down by type, type of data and years.
17. Spain has seventeen regional governments, known as Comunidades Autónomas, and two municipal governments, known as Ciudades Autónomas, that administer government programs on the Spanish mainland and islands and in the two Spanish possessions on the North African coast, respectively.
18. The respective laws, "The Public Administration Contract Law," June 16, 2000, and the "Royal Decree 1098," October 12, 2001, require the government to conduct competitive bidding on all contracts, not only architectural projects.
19. The competitions organized by Europan are open to all European architects under the age of forty. For the 2005–06 cycle, nineteen competitions have been organized. For further information see www.europan-europe.com.
20. For statistics regarding Spanish students studying abroad, see http://www.mec.es/educa/ccuniv/erasmus/imagenes/estadisticas/05_SM.pdf.
21. See John D. Hoag, *History of World Architecture: Islamic Architecture* (Milan: Electa, 1973), p. 46.
22. Embassy of Spain in the United States, "The Spanish Constitution," http://www.spainemb.org/information/constitucionin.htm. For the sections quoted here, see art. 2, sec. 1, and art. 10 and art. 20, sec. 1, respectively.
23. Ronald Hilton, "Spain: The Valle de los Caidos," World Association of International Studies, Stanford University, http://wais.stanford.edu/Spain/spain_1thevalledeloscaidos73103.html.
24. To compare the best and worst works of architecture from the Franco period, see Gabriel Ruíz Cabrero's *The Modern in Spain: Architecture after 1948* (Cambridge, Mass., and London: The MIT Press, 2001) and Gabriel Ureña's *Arquitectura y urbanística civil y militar en el período de la autarquía (1936–45): Análisis, cronología y textos* (Madrid: Istmo D. L., 1979).
25. The three authors are now practicing as two separate entities, AMP Arquitectos and Fernando Martín Menis. Mariola Merino Martín has collaborated with the former on the realization of the project.
26. Crow, *The Root and the Flower*, p. 9.
27. The term Bilbao effect is a clear and intended evocation of Beaubourg effect, a term coined by Jean Baudrillard to describe the far-reaching impact of the construction of Centre Beaubourg in Paris in 1977. Although the former term achieved wide currency soon after Gehry's building was finished, it is not clear who first used it.
28. Atkinson, *A History of Spain and Portugal*, p. 28.
29. Ibid., p. 29.
30. See Josh Cook, *The Conquest of Hispania and the Province of Tarraconensis*, http://www.usd.edu/~clehmann/pir/tarracon.htm. Among smaller towns and villages, the Via Augusta passed through the then small Colonia Julia Augusta Faventia Paterna Barcino (Barcelona), Tarraco (Tarragona), Carthago Nova (Cartagena), Corduba (Córdoba), and Hispalis (Sevilla) before reaching Gades (Cádiz).
31. Atkinson, *A History of Spain and Portugal*, p. 83. The number of towns receiving *fueros* increased as the Reconquest proceeded. From the eighth through the eleventh century approximately sixty were given, with ten times as many given in the next two centuries.
32. Miguel de Unamuno, "The Spirit of Castile," in *Essays and Soliloquies*, trans. J. E. Crawford Flitch (New York: Alfred A. Knopf, 1925), p. 33.
33. Statistics regarding ancient Roman cities and their current-day populations were obtained by comparing the data presented in César Carreras Monfort's "A New Perspective for the Demographic Study of Roman Spain," in *Revista de Historia da Arte e Arqueologia*, no. 2 (1995–96), pp. 59–82, with 2004 population figures from the Instituto Nacional de Estadística, http://www.ine.es (go to the English-language version of the website and follow the path Demography and Population/Population figures/Municipal register: Official population figures since 1996/Population figures by municipalities, islands, provinces, and autonomous communities). The regional populations of the largest cities were also increased to reflect the figures found on www.mongabay.com/igapo/Spain.htm.
34. See Cook, *Conquest of Hispania*.
35. Crow, *The Root and the Flower*, p. 56.
36. This figure was extrapolated from statistical data found on Instituto Nacional de Estadística, "Construcción de viviendas por tipo de vivienda y años," http://www.ine.es. To access this information go to the English-language version of the website and follow the path Industry and construction/Construction statistics/Main results/Construcción de viviendas por tipo de vivienda y años.
37. Luis Fernández-Galiano, "Especie Protegida," *Arquitectura Viva*, no. 100 (2005): 27.
38. Before finally being established in Madrid, the capital was essentially wherever the king and his court resided, having recently been located in Toledo, Segovia, and Valladolid.
39. Tzara quoted in Arthur C. Danto, *The Abuse of Beauty: Aesthetics and the Concept of Art* (Chicago: Open Court, 2003), p. 139.
40. Anthony Vidler, *The Architectural Uncanny: Essays in the Modern Unhomely* (Cambridge, Mass.: The MIT Press, 1992), p. 219.
41. Henry-Russell Hitchcock, Jr., and Philip Johnson, *The International Style: Architecture since 1922* (New York: W. W. Norton & Co., 1932), pp. 30–34. The book featured Mies's Barcelona Pavilion and briefly noted Labayen y Aizpurua's 1929 Yacht Club in San Sebastián, pp. 183–84 and 169, respectively.
42. Ricardo Bofill and six other Spanish architects, all of whom came of age as the International Style began to wind down, were represented in Portoghesi's exhibition: Guillermo Vázquez Consuegra of Sevilla, Francisco Biurrun Salanueva of Navarra, and Pep Bonet, Christian Cirrici, Lluís Clotet, and Oscar Tusquets Blanca of Barcelona.
43. Rem Koolhaas, "Less Is More," in *S, M, L, XL* (New York: Monacelli Press, 1995), pp. 47–61.
44. Miguel de Unamuno, "Some Arbitrary Reflections Upon Europeanization," in *Essays and Soliloquies*, trans. J. E. Crawford Flitch (New York: Alfred A. Knopf, 1925), p. 52.
45. Ibid., p. 53.

Projects

The following section contains documentation of thirty-five projects that are or soon will be under construction across Spain. Each project is accompanied by a short descriptive text. Opening this section and interspersed throughout is a panoramic survey of eighteen works recently constructed throughout the country, presented in six groups of three, all but one having been finished since 2000. These built works are accompanied by the year of their completion. Roland Halbe photographed the completed projects.

Principal architects and collaborators are listed in the heading, followed by the firm's name. When appropriate, project names have been translated into English. The map that appears in each heading indicates the location of that project. In some cases, in addition to the city a province is named to help locate lesser-known places.

Soccer Stadium (2003)

Barakaldo, Vizcaya

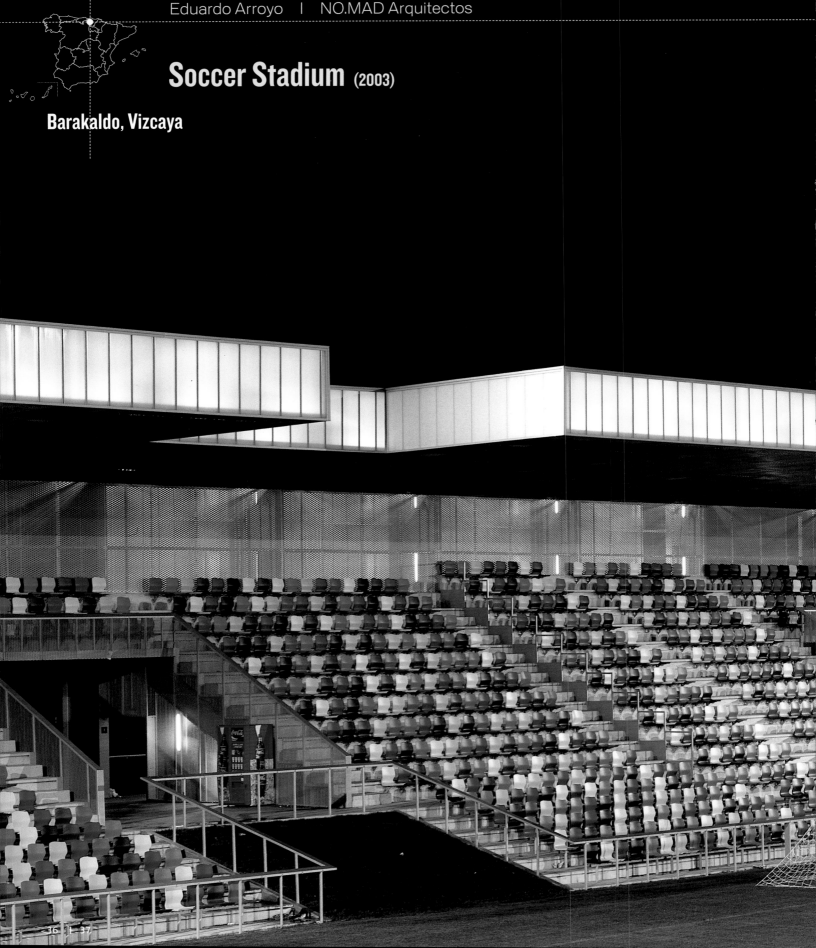

Barajas Airport Terminals (2006)

Madrid

Valleaceron Chapel (2000)

Almadenejos, Ciudad Real

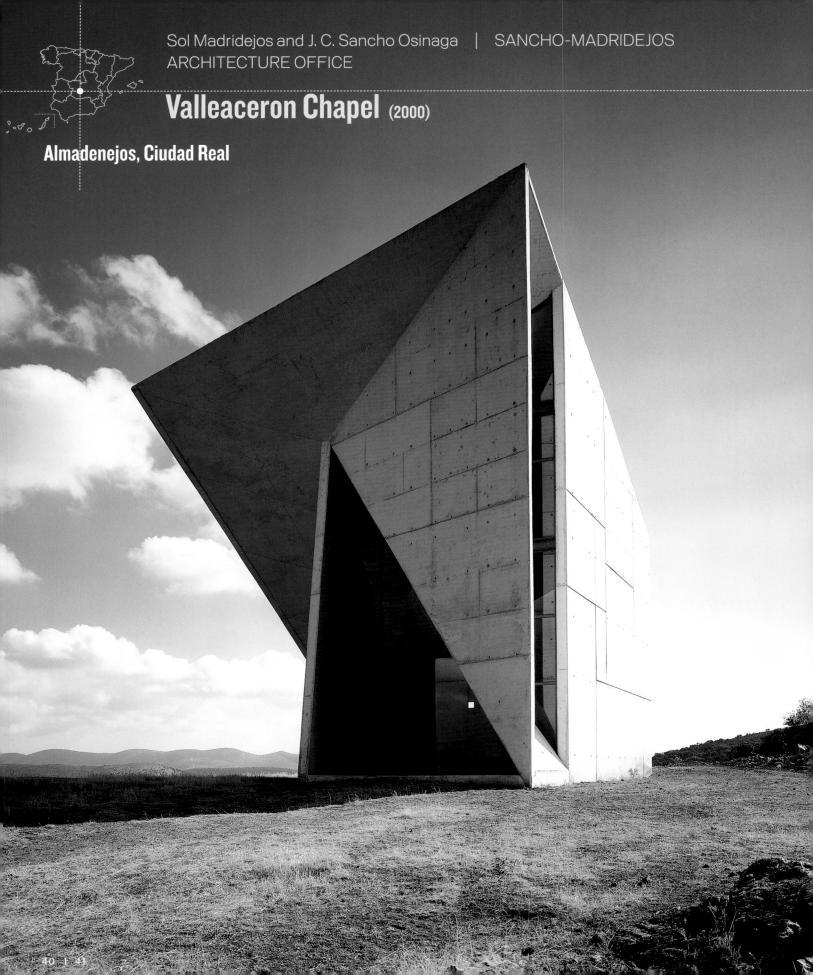

Museum of Cantabria

Santander

Emilio Tuñón and Luis M. Mansilla's winning scheme for the Museum of Cantabria in Santander is an artificial topography that creates a voluminous museum for the area's history and art. Santander, located on Spain's central northern coast, is a rather typical regional capital. In an effort to draw greater tourist and cultural attention, the city has embarked on several large building projects, including a government building by Rafael Moneo and a large athletics stadium by Franco y Palao.

The architects draw inspiration from the Cantabrian Mountains, one of the region's most notable features. The mountains provide a picturesque backdrop to the museum, and Mansilla and Tuñón's design formally references the distinctive peaks through a cluster of jagged concrete shafts. The shafts are extruded to further exaggerate the scheme the architects conceive of as a false geography, giving an overall impression of something abstract yet vaguely familiar.

Once inside, the shafts become soaring overhead channels. Periodically punctured with cutouts, they function as oversize dormer windows, letting light pour inside to the main entry space. This dramatic vestibule and the galleries on the same level are where the museum is to display its art collection. Tucked below, in a more intimate subterranean level, will be the historical collection. The building's formal clusters create a matrix of cellular galleries that can be partitioned or left open as needed. Though the formal genesis is rather untraditional for a museum, the resulting floor plans lend themselves nicely to a traditional treatment of a museum layout.

The architects often imbue their buildings with a metaphorical quality, an approach particularly evident here. In abandoning a more conventional museum typology Mansilla and Tuñón create an entirely new and highly innovative setting, making the Museum of Cantabria both a sly representation of its surroundings and a singular viewing experience.

—Peter Christensen

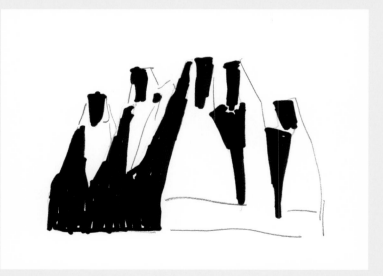

ABOVE: Sketch
OPPOSITE: Rendered view of entry plaza

Aerial view

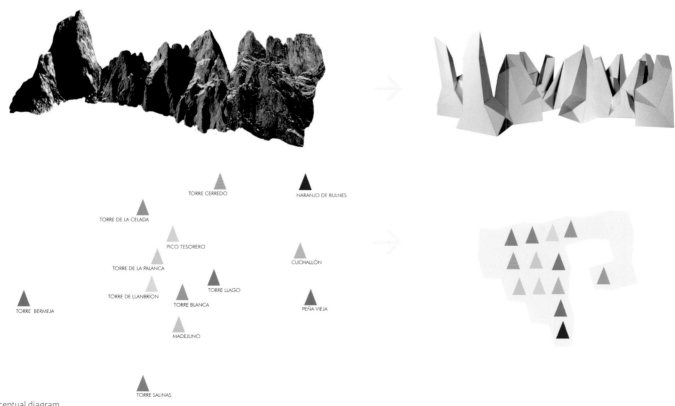

TORRE CERREDO

NARANJO DE BULNES

TORRE DE LA CELADA

PICO TESORERO

CUCHALLÓN

TORRE DE LA PALANCA

TORRE LLAGO

TORRE BERMEJA

TORRE DE LLANBRÍON

TORRE BLANCA

PEÑA VIEJA

MADEJUNO

TORRE SALINAS

Conceptual diagram

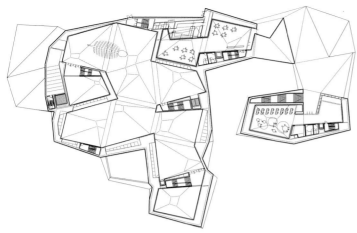

Art museum plan, ground floor

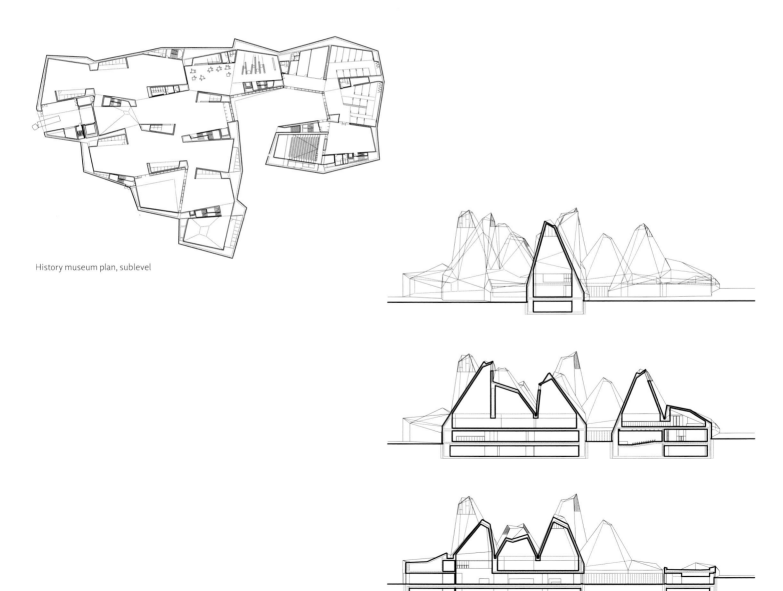

History museum plan, sublevel

East–west sections

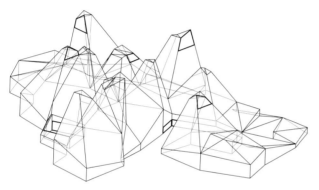 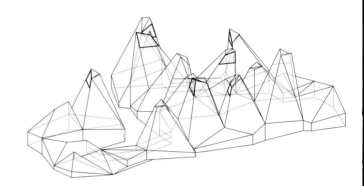

Isometric volume diagrams

Sectional rendering from north

Rendered view from north

Peter Eisenman | Eisenman Architects

City of Culture of Galicia

Santiago de Compostela

The City of Culture of Galicia, designed by Peter Eisenman, sits atop a hillside two miles east of Santiago de Compostela, overlooking the city's medieval center. The impressive 52-acre development will be a new forum for cultural and intellectual exchange between visitors from across the globe in a city that has been a destination for Christian pilgrims since the ninth century.

The design began with the superimposition of three plans. Two of them, the medieval street pattern of Santiago and the topographic mapping of the hillside site, are extracted from the local context. The third is an abstract Cartesian grid laid over the site. These layers are then scrambled by an architectural code that acts upon the indexed plans to rewrite their former logic, torquing and transforming the two-dimensional information into volumetric mass. The resulting construction of sculpted land emerging from the hillside concerns itself with surface and spatial movement rather than lines or planes. In the words of the architect, "The result is an organicism in which geometry and space become a single continuous flow."

Like a shell, which is the symbol for Santiago's namesake, Saint James, the plan of the project is structured around five rib-like pedestrian streets that striate the site. These paths pass through the complex, dividing its form into volumes that accommodate a

periodicals archive, a library, a theater, an administration building, a museum of Galician history, and a center for new technologies. The internal order of each building in the complex is distinct from its molded external surface, which is clad in native stone.

In contrast to the organization found in the city center of Santiago and other European cities where buildings and street patterns and topography are differentiated, here these elements merge into a smooth, continuous fabric. As a whole, the City of Culture of Galicia is a form that exists both of and beyond the city, incorporating Santiago's history while offering a model for future architectural production.

—Alexandra Quantrill

Model

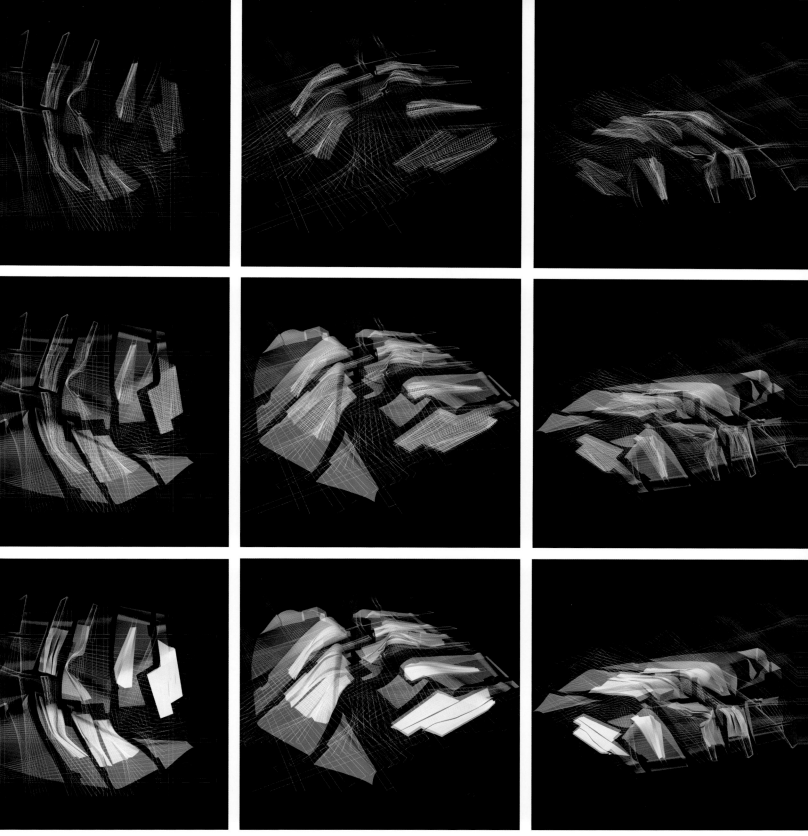

Deformation diagram

Site plan

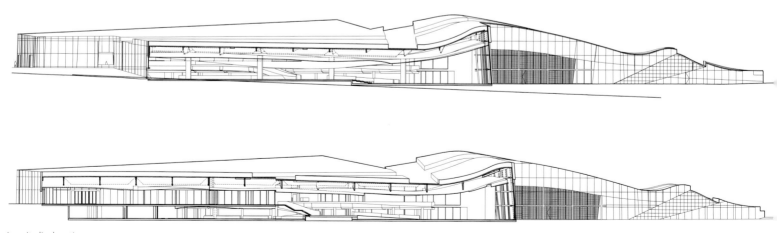

Longitudinal sections

Transverse sections

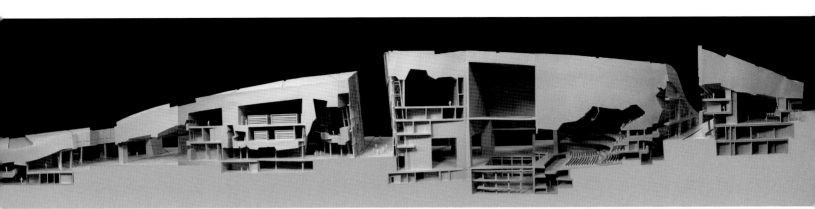

Sectional model

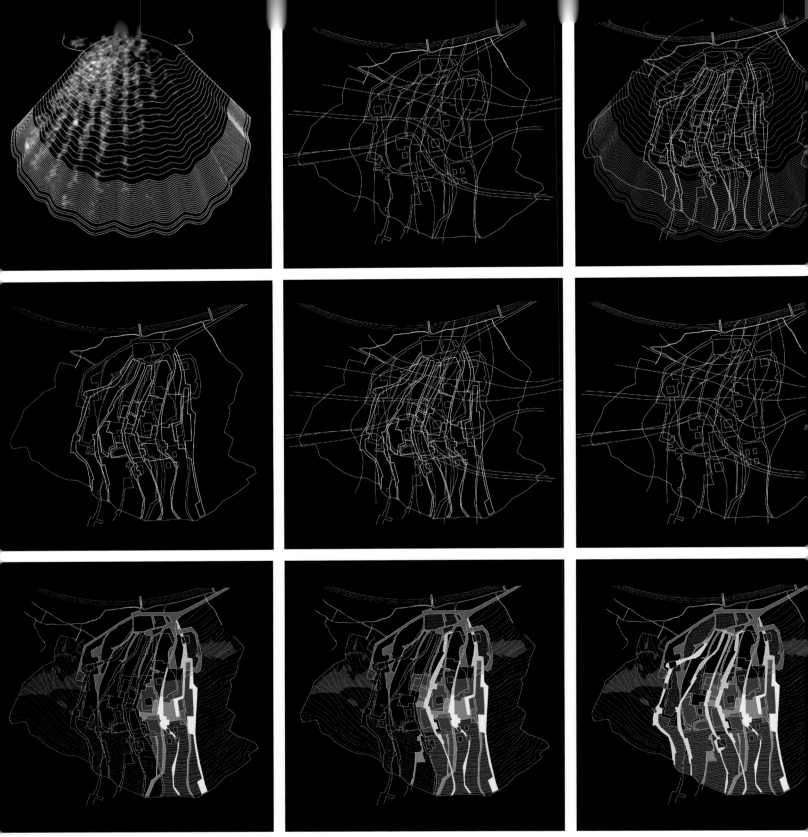

Diagram showing site development

Construction photos

Edificio Zaida

Granada

Modern day Granada, like many of Spain's historic cities, is a somber collage of architectural epochs. Nestled in its city center is an important public meeting place, Plaza Fuente de Batallas. This triangular park negotiates the junction of two main avenues: Carrera del Genil, an eighteenth-century tree-lined boulevard, and Acera del Darro, the former bed of the Darro River. Before the turn of the last century, the river was filled in to create what is now a bustling commercial thoroughfare. Portuguese architect Álvaro Siza's Edificio Zaida is located along the northern edge of the plaza. The Zaida is part of a master plan for the area, which includes the complete remodeling of Casa Patio, a late-nineteenth-century house to the west.

Siza negotiates the disparate conditions of the site with ease, lending the corner a much-needed sense of unity through his individual treatment of the building's three facades. The first three levels of the building, which constitute commercial and office space,

are clad in a local Sierra Elvira stone. This same stone also paves the surrounding sidewalks, giving the building the appearance that it is a vertical continuation of the urban floor. Starting at the fourth story, where the residential units begin, are three more levels that are finished in simple white plaster, also a common local material. The western facade, along the quiet Carrera del Genil, looks toward the Alhambra, Granada's architectural treasure. On this side, the upper three levels of the Zaida are carved back, deferring to the commanding presence of the vista beyond by providing several patios from which to view it. The plaza side of the building, with its two towerlike forms that emerge on the fourth story, references the Neoclassical traditions of adjacent residential buildings. The terrace formed between the towers is a miniaturized version of the commodious central courtyard often found in the housing typology being referenced. The third facade, on the busy Acera del Darro, is a strict grid of windows that echoes

its twentieth-century counterparts along the relatively young thoroughfare. Views out toward these varied contexts are framed by rectangular windows or are seen from panoramic roof decks, creating a dy-namic interior space from which to observe the city.

The Edifico Zaida is a testament to the power of a facade to convey a building's intentions. Siza has responded to existing street conditions by creating a triptych— three panels with specific references and strategies that come together to enclose a place from which to understand the city's many layers. Despite the varied contexts, the structure as a whole is unified by the elegant materiality and clarity of intent, an unmistakable characteristic of the architect's work.

—PC

Northeast elevation

Northwest elevation

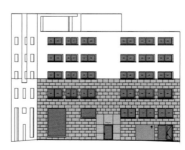

Southwest elevation

Aerial view from plaza

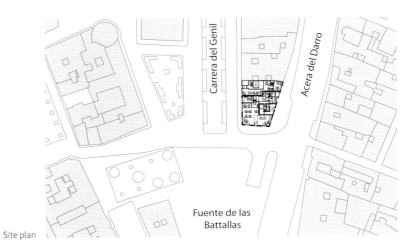
Site plan

Carrera del Genil

Acera del Darro

Fuente de las
Battallas

Floor 5

Roof

Floor 3

Floor 4

Floor 1

Floor 2

Basement

Ground floor

Plans

View north from street

1

2

3

4   5

1–3: Longitudinal sections; 4 and 5: Transverse sections

View of northeast corner

View of terrace

View looking north from roof deck

View looking southwest from roof deck

Jürgen Mayer H.   I   J.MAYER H.

Metropol Parasol

Sevilla

In contrast to notable architectural construction at the outer edges of Sevilla for the 1992 World's Fair, the medieval urban fabric of the city's center has remained largely untouched. Within the densely packed fabric of the old city, the Plaza de la Encarnación, left empty after its nineteenth-century market structures were dismantled in 1973, is one of the few open spaces. A parking lot occupied the space until plans for an underground garage necessitated excavations beneath the surface. When Roman ruins were found under the plaza, Sevilla's government had to reconsider the significance of this pocket of land. It launched an international design competition for a project intended to generate the kind of social exchange and commercial activity that the plaza had once provided the city. In addition, local authorities wished to use this new project to assert Sevilla's identity as a thriving contemporary city, much like Frank Gehry's Guggenheim Museum has done for Bilbao.

Metropol Parasol, Jürgen Mayer H.'s winning scheme, comprises six organically shaped "parasols" that reach to 90 feet above the Roman ruins, which have been left intact and will become a public museum. The trunks of these towering forms, which conceal vertical access to the museum below and to a roof terrace above, are carefully positioned to avoid sensitive archaeological artifacts and to guide pedestrian movement across the site. The mushroom-shaped growths shade the open plaza below, where a raised platform sits atop the new market hall and creates a stage for public events. At the roof level, observation platforms and a café nestled within the canopies afford sweeping vistas of Sevilla.

The curvaceous forms of the parasols are constructed of laminated timber in a three-dimensional grid—a merging of the orthogo-

nal with the organic. The appearance of this extruded lattice will oscillate between opacity and transparency depending on shifting conditions of natural and artificial light; the shadows it casts throughout the year will also range from gridded and porous to completely solid. Its undulating roofline distinguishes Metropol Parasol from the surrounding urban context and announces a vital new presence in the heart of the old city.

—AQ

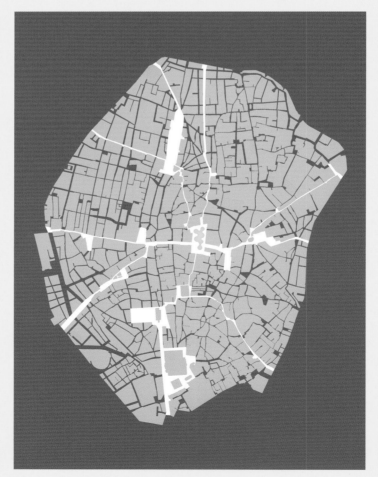

Site plan

Rendered view from southwest

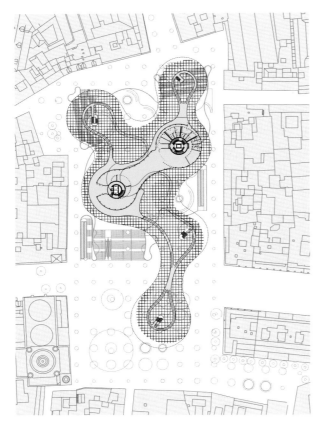

Plan, plaza level three

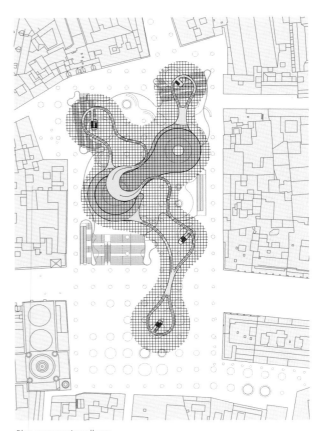

Plan, panoramic walkway

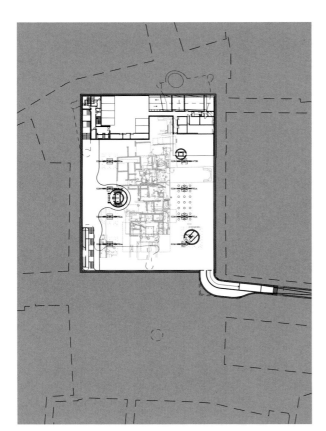

Plan, subterranean plaza level

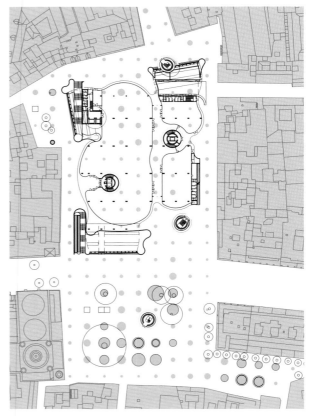

Plan, plaza level one

Rendered view into archaeological site, market, and elevated plaza from Calle Imagen

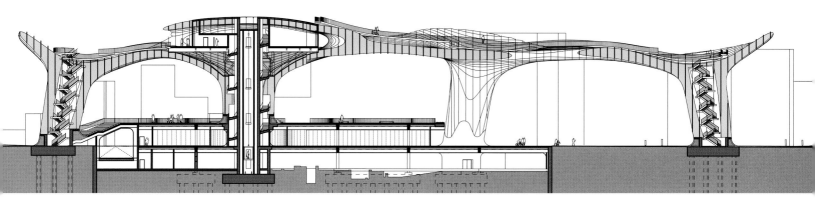

North–south section

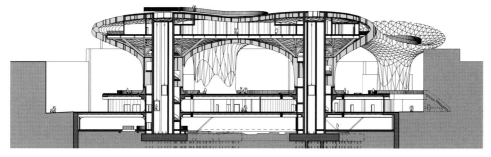

East–west section

Rendered view of concert event on plaza level two

Rendered view of panoramic walkway from south

manuel bailo + rosa rull

City Hall Facade

Manresa, Barcelona

Manuel Bailo and Rosa Rull's winning proposal for a new facade on Manresa's city hall is a small-scale project with large ambitions, giving the building a much-needed facelift. Manresa, located in Barcelona's northern outskirts, sits at the foot of the Montserrat Mountains. Composed of pink sedimentary rock, the mountains, with their unusual jagged formations, are one of Spain's most striking geological sites. The hall mediates between Manresa's main plaza to the east and the mountainous backdrop to the west across the Cardener River. The existing nineteenth-century stone building failed to capitalize on the tremendous westerly view, instead privileging the more public functions associated with the plaza.

In an effort to exploit the vista and to restabilize the western facade—part of which had begun to decay—the architects have strategically carved out approximately one-third of this side of the building, spanning all five of its levels, eliminating the structure's weakest portions. A steel frame restabilizes the wall within the carved section and functions as the skeleton from which several triangulated wood and glass planes emerge. Enclosed within this growth swelling from the building's old facade is a stairway, which will function as the main vertical circulation. By rerouting the circulation to this western facade, the architects have orchestrated a procession through the building that automatically engages the view that previously had remained hidden. The seemingly arbitrary geometry of the planes is an improvisational technique that grafts and mutates according to contextual cues, including, in this case, the existing frame, the enclosure of the stairwell,

and maximization of particular viewing points, namely at the stairwell landings.

As many of Spain's historic buildings undergo expansion or renovation, the strategies architects bring to these contexts have become increasingly varied. Here, the architects take a decidedly adventurous approach, addressing the flaws of an older design while making no reference to its historical architectural language or traditional materials. That said, the addition takes on a parasitic relationship with its host, unable to exist without it. Bailo and Rull's bold addition is a candid and unapologetic improvement to the building upon which it rests.

—PC

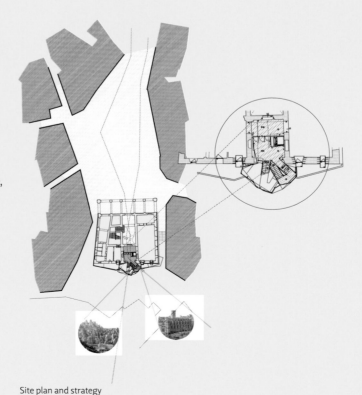

Site plan and strategy

Rendered view of facade from southwest

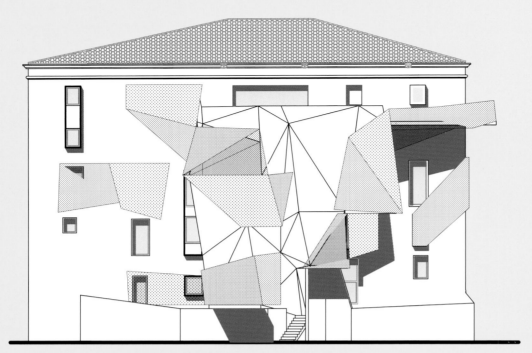

Elevation

Computer studies, southeast facade

Site section

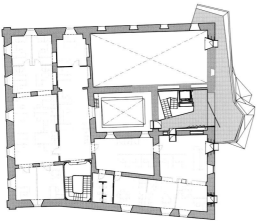

Plan, floor 5

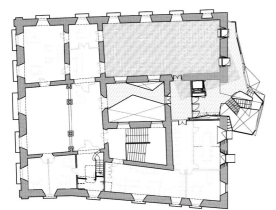

Plan, floor 3

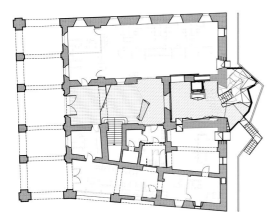

Plan, ground floor

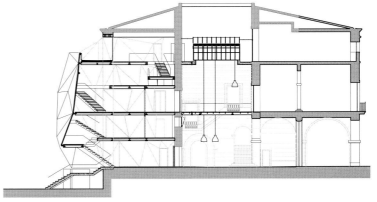

Section through entry

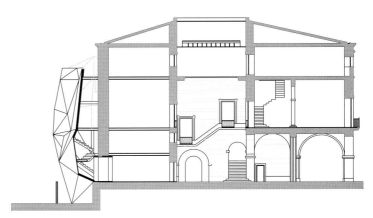

Section through courtyard

Alejandro Zaera-Polo and Farshid Moussavi | Foreign Office Architects (FOA)
with Antonio Maqueríe Arquitectos y Asociados

Municipal Theater and Auditorium

Torrevieja, Alicante

Torrevieja, located on Spain's southeast coast along the Costa Blanca, is primarily a tourist destination known for its beautiful beaches and mild climate. The Municipal Theater and Auditorium by Alejandro Zaera-Polo and Farshid Moussavi is one of the many current projects intended to expand the town's profile from a touristic center to a cultural one.

The building is situated on a corner site within the town center and incorporates an adjacent public plaza. Its design mediates between two opposing conditions: completing the corner of the city block and inserting itself as an autonomous formal object into the urban fabric. The monolithic volume, inspired by the black box of the theater, appears as if an incision were cut into its mass to create a seamless continuum between the foyer and the plaza. This gesture exposes the sloping floor of the theater while extending the outdoor square beneath the building. Large glass partitions create a striking contrast to the solidity of the local limestone that clads the rest of the building.

Once inside visitors can either descend to a sunken café or ascend via ramps to the theater. The stage was designed for maximum flexibility and will accommodate a variety of productions, from traditional theater and cinema to more avant-garde media performances. The seating for the audience is situated on a single sloping level, rather than in tiers, so as to maintain an intimate proximity to the stage. Rehearsal and production rooms are above.

—Tina diCarlo

Rendered view looking toward entry from sunken lobby

Rendered view looking toward entry plaza

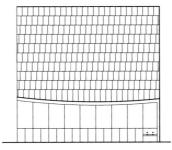

Plaza elevation

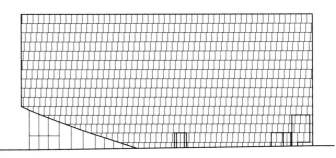

Street elevation

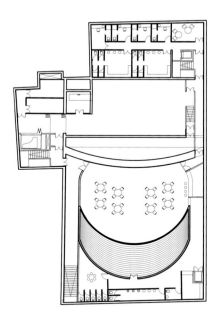

Plan, sublevel

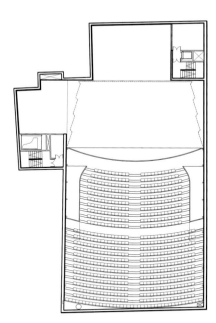

Plan, upper level

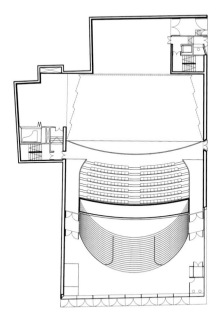

Plan, stage level

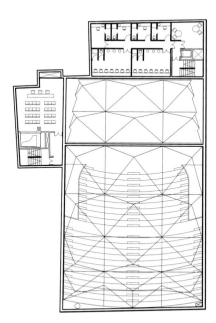

Plan, top level

Model, view across entry plaza

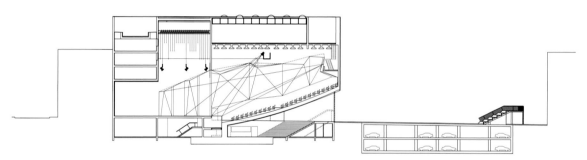

Longitudinal section

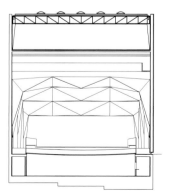

Transverse section through stage

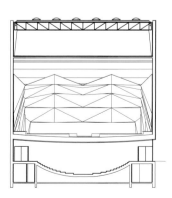

Transverse section through lobby

Rendered view looking into sunken lobby from entry

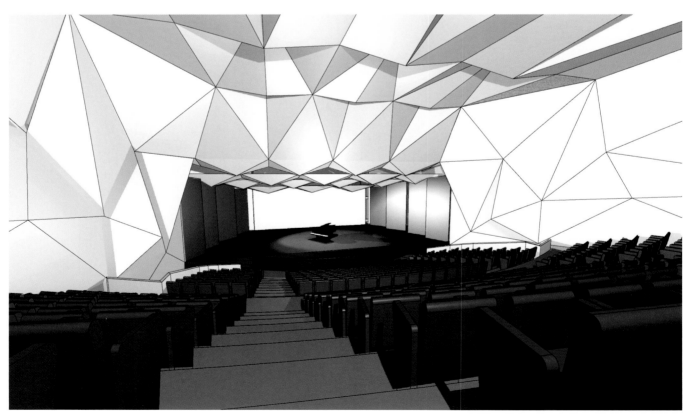

Rendered view of auditorium

Model, with facade cutaway

Construction photo, plaza side

Construction photo, view from sunken lobby

Museum of Andalucía

Granada

Few architects have the chance to revisit the site of one of their works and further the story that it tells. This is not the case for Alberto Campo Baeza, whose Museum of Andalucía is sited one block north of his seminal Caja Granada (2001), a savings bank on the outskirts of Granada. The bank building is a large cubic volume that rests on a plinth designed to create a level platform over the gentle slope of the site. Within the volume a dramatic eight-story atrium receives light that is filtered through a variety of mechanisms, including an exterior brise-soleil, a honeycomb roof, and a travertine and glass facade. The architect calls this space an "impluvium of light," a clear reference to Andalucía's Roman architectural heritage.

For the museum, which will present historic and artistic artifacts from the region's past, Campo Baeza creates another plinth and aligns it with the one across the street. This time, however, the architect has chosen to excavate it rather than place a structure on it. The result is a three-story subterranean building whose centerpiece is a spacious, light-filled ellipsoidal courtyard. Two spiral ramps connect the three levels, allowing visitors to move in and out of the courtyard as they circulate between galleries. At the northernmost end of the building arises a narrow eight-story administrative tower, again referencing the Caja Granada in the duplication of its height and width.

Viewed from the top of one its ramps, the museum functions as a platform for viewing the Caja Granada and the Sierra Nevada Mountains beyond. The procession downward to the sunken patio affords the viewer an opportunity to escape that context while still being outside. Unlike the atrium, or impluvium, of the Caja Granada, the central courtyard of the museum functions as its inverse, forging a space where ample natural light can coexist with a sense of refuge and contemplation.

—PC

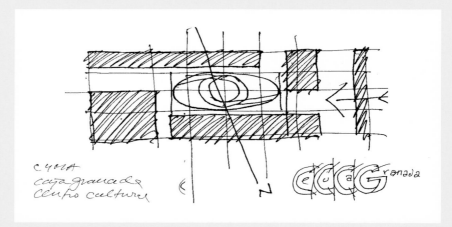

ABOVE: Sketch
OPPOSITE: Rendered view looking south toward the Caja Granada

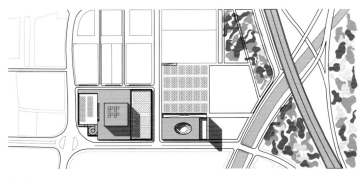

Site plan

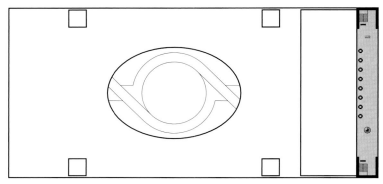

Typical plan, upper levels

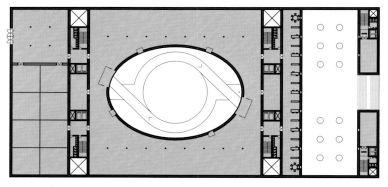

Plan, entry level

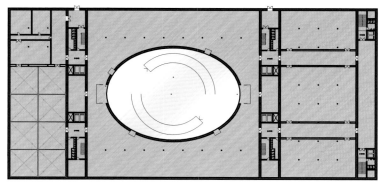

Plan, courtyard level

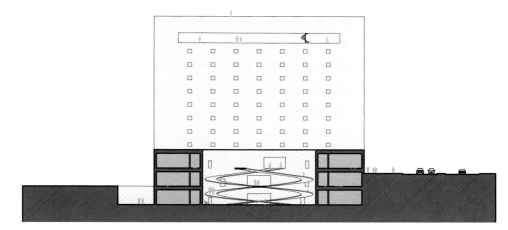

Transverse section

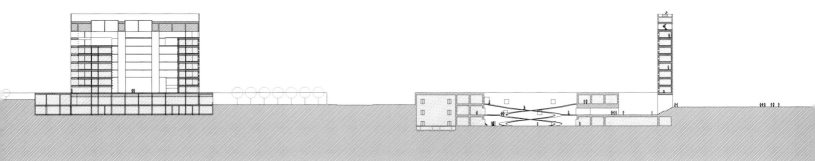

Site section through Caja Granada and museum

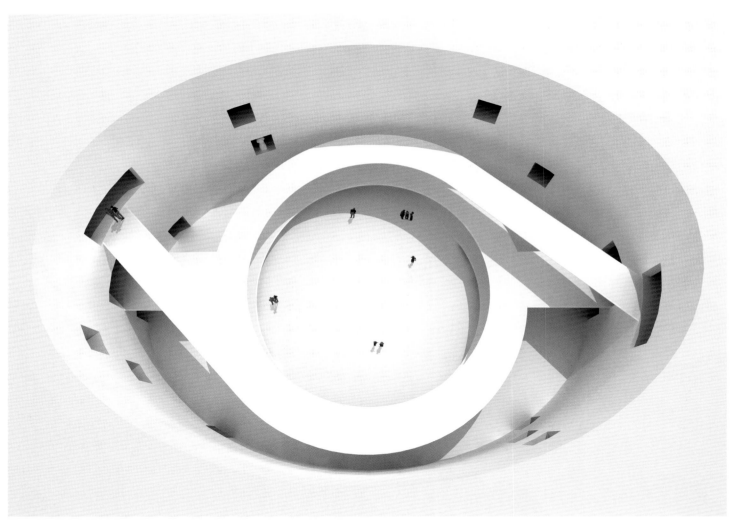

Rendered view looking down into courtyard

Rendered view of sunken patio

Iñaki Ábalos, Juan Herreros, Renata Sentkiewicz, Joaquin Casariego, and
Elsa Guerra | Abalos&Herreros with CASARIEGO/GUERRA, arquitectos

Woermann Complex (2005)

Las Palmas de Gran Canaria

Social Services Center (2003)

Barcelona

Museo Nacional Centro de Arte Reina Sofía Expansion (2005

Madrid

Relaxation Park

Torrevieja, Alicante

Torrevieja is a typical resort town on Spain's Costa Blanca. Stretching along the eastern coastline from Castellon to Almeria, the region is known for its remarkable Mediterranean beaches. In the summer months the town's population multiplies by a factor of ten, largely due to tourists from other European countries. The town also has two inland lakes with a curious pinkish tint due to a high concentration of sea salt and bacteria, and because of this the mud from the lakeshore is believed to be beneficial for health and beauty. Toyo Ito's Relaxation Park, part of an effort to shift some tourist activity from the beachfront to the lakeshore, is a place for such spa treatments.

The park has been landscaped to mimic gently sloping sand dunes. Three shell-shaped structures are embedded along the dunes. Each shell has a different purpose: one is a restaurant, one an information center with locker facilities, and one an open-air pool. The basis of the shells' forms are cocoonlike spiral frames. These skeletons weave together the main structural elements, which consist of steel rods and a secondary system of timber joists. The frame is then clad with plywood in areas requiring closure and left unclad in areas

that do not. The result is a soft exoskeleton in which the skin and bones are alternately exposed. The floors are hung from the frame, giving the structure added rigidity.

The resulting organic, undulating forms offer both intimate and more generous spaces, allowing the buildings to accommodate a variety of both private and public functions. Together the three structures evoke an image of organisms in different moments of regeneration, echoing the performative and experiential purposes of the park.

—PC

ABOVE: Aerial view
OPPOSITE: Aerial rendering from south

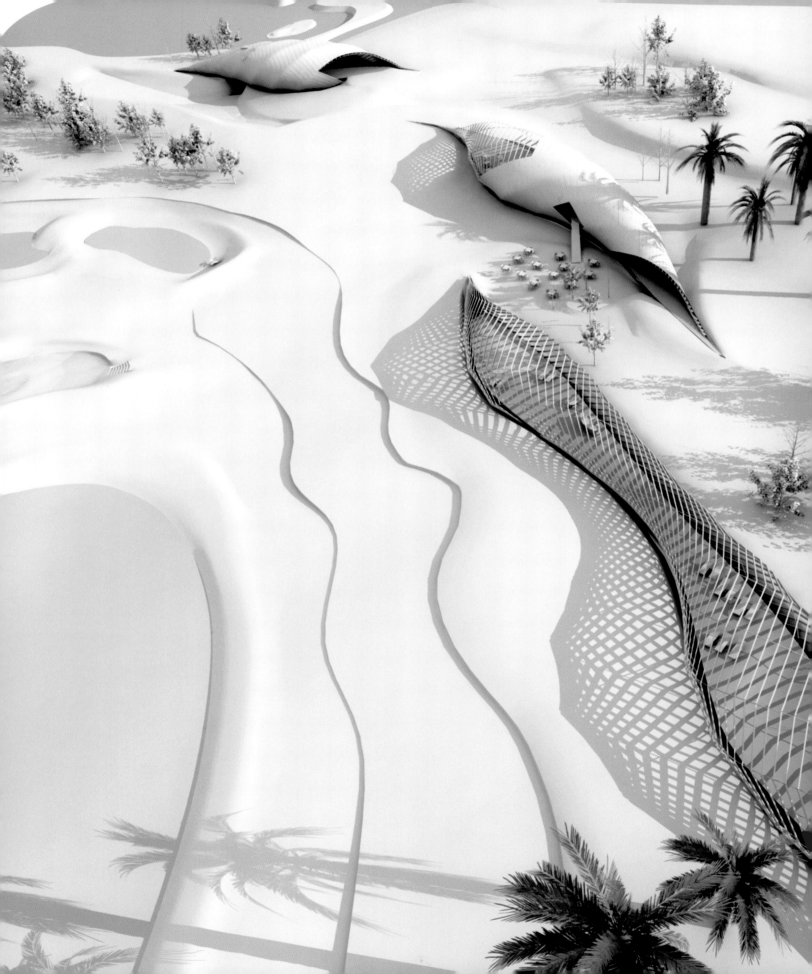

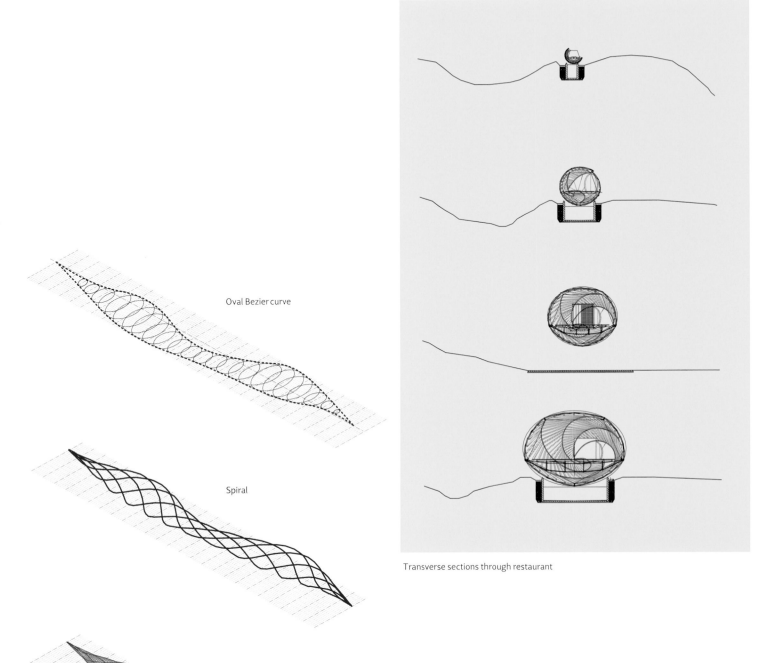

Oval Bezier curve

Spiral

Timber purlin

Diagram showing form and construction scheme

Transverse sections through restaurant

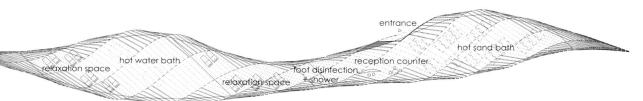

relaxation space

hot water bath

relaxation space

foot disinfection + shower

reception counter

entrance

hot sand bath

Open-air bath plan

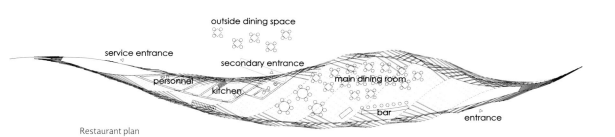

outside dining space

service entrance

secondary entrance

personnel

kitchen

main dining room

bar

entrance

Restaurant plan

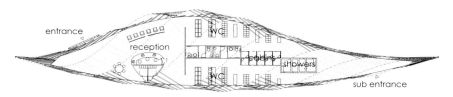

entrance

reception

WC

WC

cabins

showers

sub entrance

Information office plan

Rendered view of spa interior

Rendered view from northwest

Construction detail showing joists

Construction photo of restaurant

Juan Domingo Santos

House in a Cherry Orchard

Granada

Conceived as part of a comprehensive land-scape proposal, the House in a Cherry Orchard by Juan Domingo Santos is situated in the agricultural terrain of Cajar in southern Spain. The project explores how urban domestic life might be relocated to the cultivated land-scape that surrounds Granada, allowing an alternative to city living without compromising the local agrarian culture.

A viable new cherry orchard has been con-structed above a preexisting one, creating an artificial topography that extends across the site like a platform. The house is nestled within this elevated ground plane, with the propor-tions of its rooms determined by the regular spacing of the trees. The rooms are positioned above, below, and coincident with the artificial ground, providing the occupant varied percep-tions of the surrounding orchard.

Reinforced concrete walls frame the hori-zontal volumes of the house, within which vertical circulation is concealed. An excavated patio slopes down from the raised orchard surface to the library, garage, and storage spaces buried within the earth. The kitchen and main living space, situated at the level of the man-made ground, define views out beneath the tree canopies while the bedrooms and a screened solarium occupy a terrace that hovers above the new orchard surface, afford-ing panoramas of the treetops.

For Domingo Santos, architectural design and the natural environment are interrelated. The pattern of perforations in the bedroom walls is derived from the ventilated tobacco-drying pavilions found in the area. As they weather, the concrete walls will develop a patina and will appear as extensions of the land-scape. The cherry trees so visible from the house reflect the changing seasons in their flowers and foliage, making the passage of time integral to this architectural experience. Domingo Santos combines a material sensibility with his concern for local ecology: "I believe that architecture has to do with all of this, how you illuminate, ventilate, and position space, but also with change, temporality, and transfor-mation of the environment."

The long-term objective of the project is to build a series of similar dwellings within a reconfigured landscape in which fences would eventually be eliminated, replaced by a network of paths and irrigation ditches that would mark individual lots. Houses would be sited in voids within the continuous cherry orchard, which could also be used as a park, thereby combining public, agricultural, and domestic space within one landscape.

—AQ

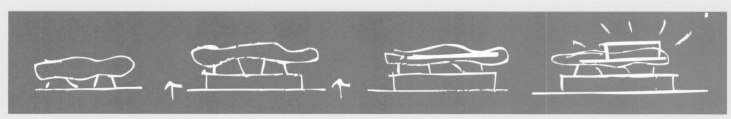

Sketch

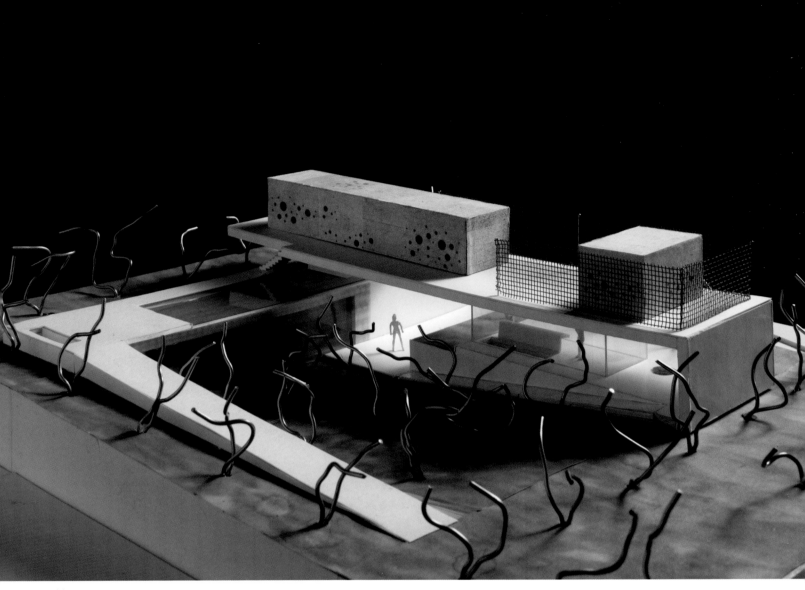

Model

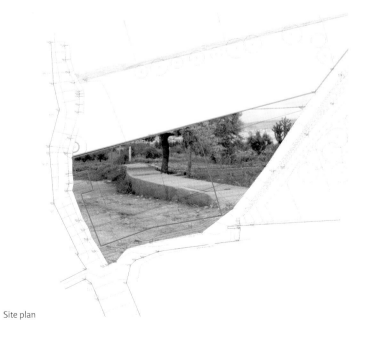

Site plan

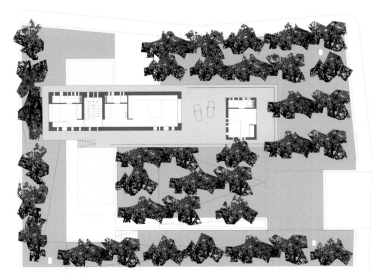

Plan, upper level

Plan, orchard level

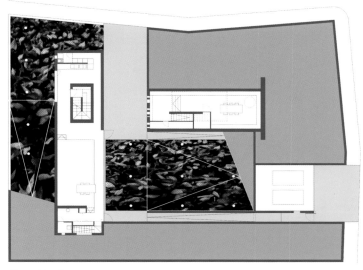

Plan, sublevel

East elevation

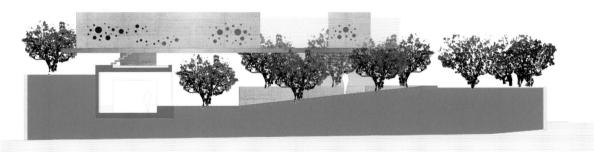

Section through orchard

Rendered view looking west over orchard

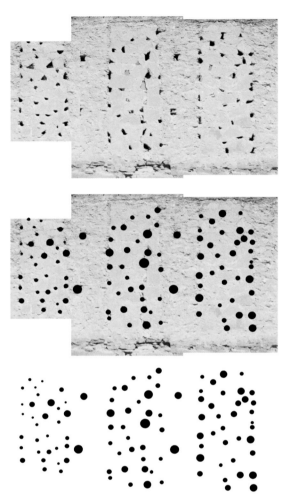

Aperture studies

View from east

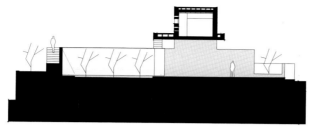

Transverse section

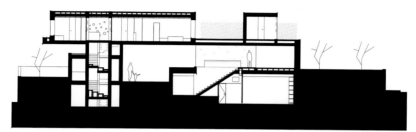

Longitudinal section

Arts Center

La Coruña

Victoria Acebo and Ángel Alonso's Arts Center in La Coruña is a prime example of how much of the new construction in Spain is bringing the arts to some unexpected outposts around the country. La Coruña, a municipality in the extreme northwest of the region of Galicia, has historically been the administrative and shipping center for the area. As much of the region's cultural activity has been focused in nearby Santiago de Compostela, La Coruña has been largely overshadowed. The project playfully melds two programs, a dance conservatory and an art museum, into a deceptively simple and unified whole.

The two components of the center, the conservatory and the museum, were conceived as autonomous bodies within a single cubic steel and glass volume. Splayed off of the central concrete circulation core like branches of a tree are several booths or boxes, each varying in size. As these spaces meet the exterior envelope, their volumetric reading becomes legible from the outside, creating a patchwork of rectangles each clad in a subtly different fashion. The volumes housing each discrete program connect, winding around each other along the building's vertical core until both programs meet in a

grand atrium. This central meeting space—made lively through brightly colored acoustic ceiling tubes and the striking double-glazed and tinted glass cladding—cleverly inverts the building's own yin-and-yang formalism and also affords a view of all interconnecting volumes.

Acebo and Alonso's concept for the project is one that begins remarkably simply and suddenly questions its own logic. The rational formal, structural, and material strategies belie the building's more colorful internal juxtapositions. The tension between hiding and revealing lends the center an unexpected personality. The culmination of this playful approach will be an exciting new cultural destination for La Coruña.

—PC

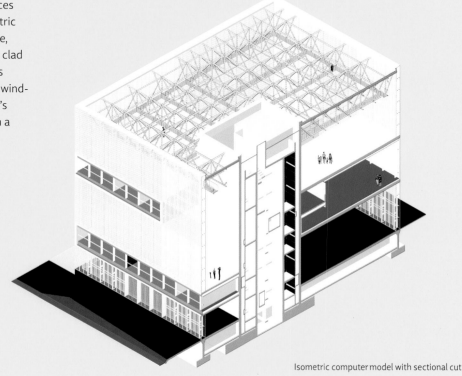

Isometric computer model with sectional cut

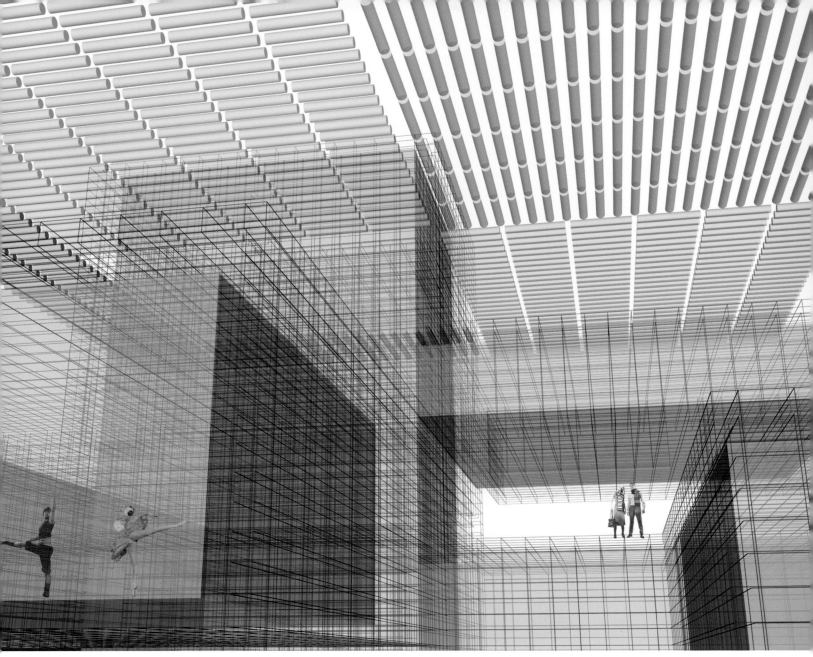

Perspective diagram of interior

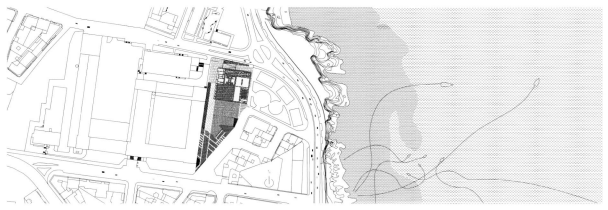

Site plan

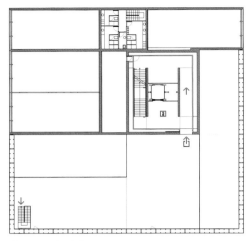

Plan, atrium level, floor 3

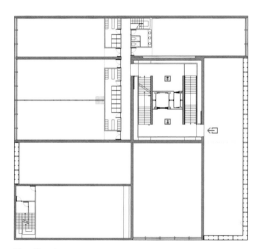

Plan, floor 2

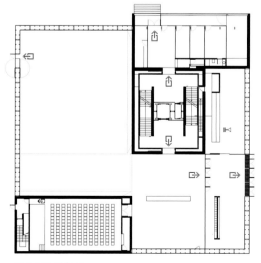

Plan, ground floor

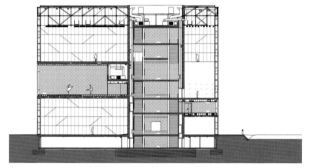

North–south section

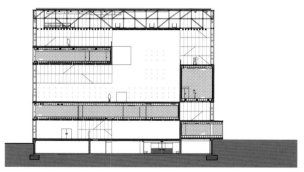

East–west section

View of north facade

View of atrium, southeast corner

View of atrium, northwest corner

Hotel Habitat

L'Hospitalet de Llobregat, Barcelona

Hotel Habitat, designed by Enric Ruiz-Geli in collaboration with Acconci Studio and Ruy Ohtake, is a funky marriage of ecology and technology. Situated alongside the Gran Via, a major vehicular thoroughfare in L'Hospitalet de Llobregat, the four-star hotel is one of a number of projects being built by prominent architects on Barcelona's outskirts, a sign of the city's increasing urban sprawl. The eleven-story hotel houses 135 rooms, a restaurant, a gym, and a roof terrace within a rectangular volume that steps back on its lower and upper three levels. Some suites on the seventh and eighth floors protrude from the volume on its southern facade, while the egress stairwell protrudes on the northern facade. Posts that jut from many of the building's corners provide the loose skeleton upon which a web rests, giving the hotel a simultaneously orthogonal and fluid profile.

The web, which comprises a dense matrix of 5,000 LEDs powered by photovoltaic cells fused together into one unit, is entirely independent from the energy grid of the volume underneath. In addition, each unit is embedded with a clock that tracks a year's worth of sunrises and sunsets, making it possible to time a cyclical reserve and release of energy. Factors such as the path and intensity of the day's sun and weather help determine what color light will be activated at night. When the lowest amount of energy has been

reserved the cell will glow red; from there it makes use of the entire light spectrum, emanating yellows, greens, and blues, finally utilizing white when there is the greatest amount of energy. At night, this luminous diurnal diagram becomes a glowing advertisement for the hotel. During the day, the shadows of the cells provide shading for up to twenty percent of the building's surface area, lowering cooling costs. Like leaves on a tree, the cells have a double function, performing a sort of photosynthesis and providing shade.

Beneath the web, small trees, plants, and pools further enhance the building's unique microclimate.

The technologies at the core of the project, the LEDs and the photovoltaic cells, are not novel in and of themselves. By merging them into a symbiotic unit, however, the architect creates new possibilities. The union of ecology, technology, and marketing makes this building an original hybrid that demands attention.

—PC

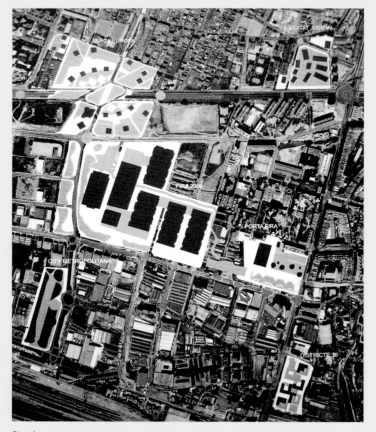

Site plan

Rendered view, nighttime

Detail of LED matrix, nighttime

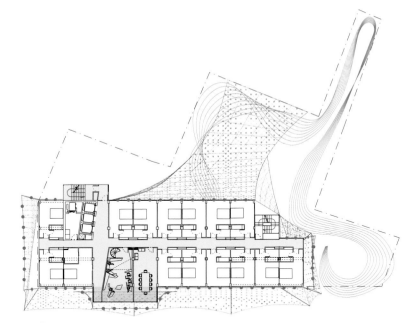

Plan, floor 7

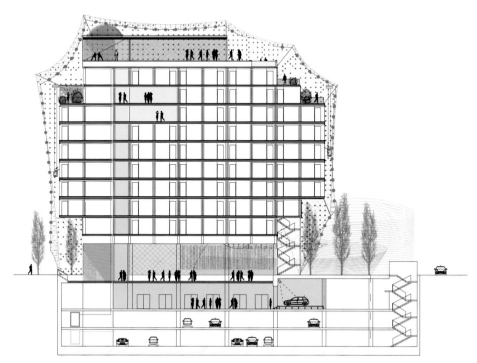

Longitudinal section

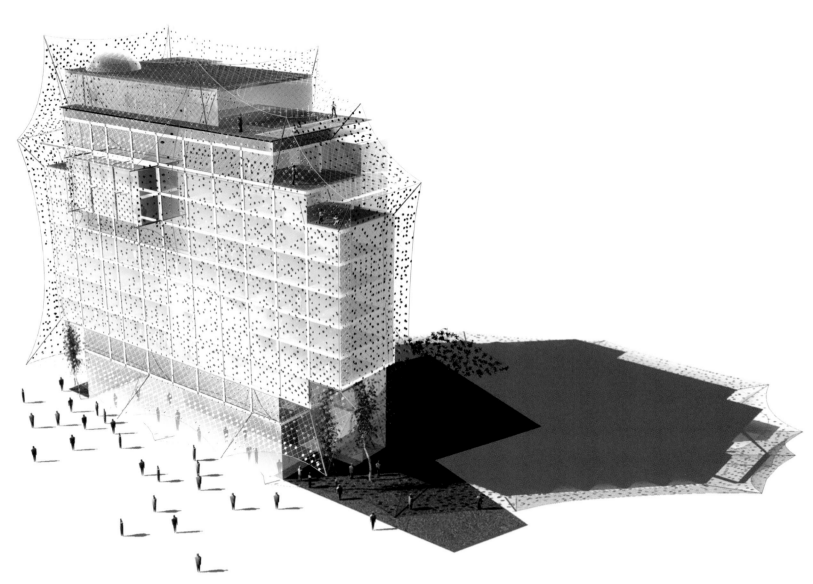

Rendered aerial view

Rendered view from across boulevard

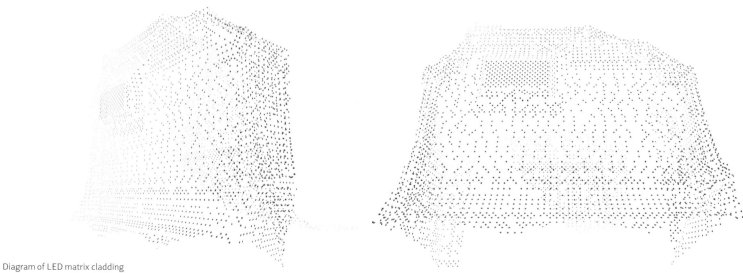

Diagram of LED matrix cladding

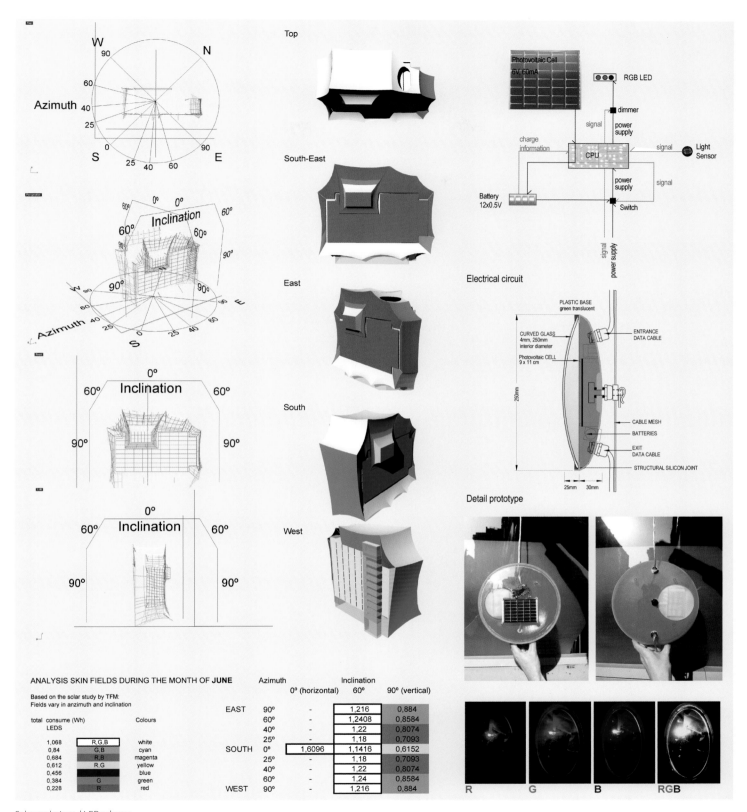

Solar analysis and LED scheme

Parador

Alcalá de Henares, Madrid

Maria José Aranguren López and José González Gallegos's Parador comprises a renovation and addition to the Old College of Saint Thomas. The full-block site is located in Alcalá de Henares, a city several kilometers north of Madrid and known as the birthplace of Miguel de Cervantes. Enclosed by a perimeter wall, the site retains the original gridded order of the former orchard, or *huerta*. Preexisting buildings include a cloister and two long factories, one that runs parallel to one side of the cloister and another, skewed at a 30-degree angle to the first, situated directly behind the cloister's rear corner.

The architects conceived the overall design to maintain the duality of an open yet contained garden and to reflect the dual nature of the complex's program: an inn and a school of hotel management. The inn occupies two-thirds of the site, with rooms located off pinwheel-shaped sunken gardens and on the second and third levels of the adjacent factory. Rooms in the new area are inspired by Japanese design while those in the factory retain a more historic character.

The school, punctuated by a series of regularly spaced sunken cubic volumes forming double-height gardens, comprises the remaining third of the site. Raised patios divide these volumes into open and covered areas below. From the street, the school is less visible than the hotel, dissolving into a horizontal platform into which classrooms, living quarters, dining rooms, and kitchens are absorbed. The school also occupies the second factory, where additional classrooms, the library, an administrative area. Living quarters are located on the second floor.

L-shaped shells cover each factory, preserving their front facades while providing a neutral design for the rear facades that filters light into the interior. A new building mirrors the existing cloister. Dining rooms, kitchens, a spa, and a fitness area are located in the cloisters. The vehicular and pedestrian entry is next to the original college in the center of the site, and parking is located below.

—TDC

Organizational diagram

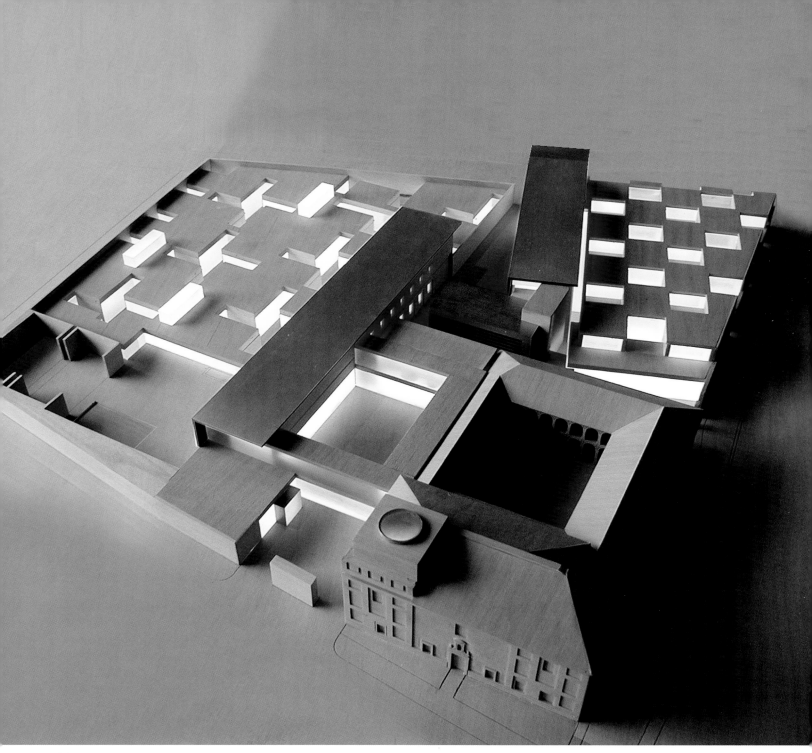

Model

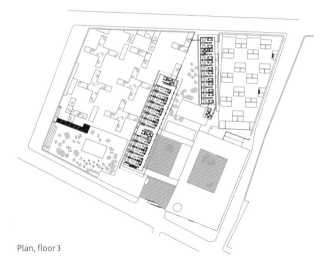

Plan, floor 3

Plan, floor 2

Plan, ground floor

Rendered view of south entry

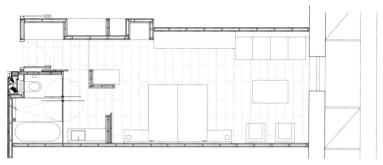

Plan, room type 1

East–west section

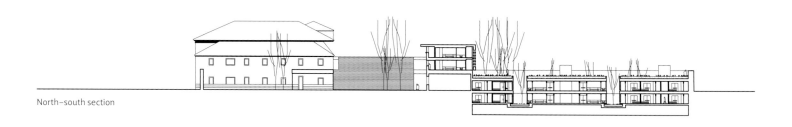

North–south section

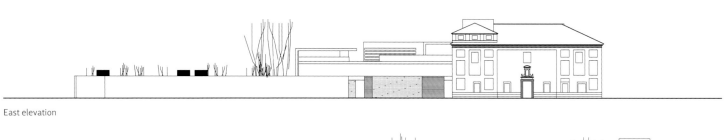

East elevation

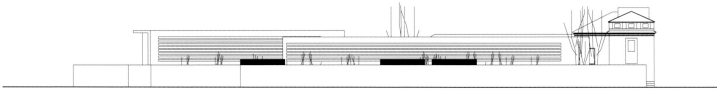

South elevation

DINING ROOM   **NEW PATIO**   DINING ROOM   **FORMER PATIO**   DINING ROOM

Sectional perspective

Rendered view of roofscape from raised patios

Rendered view of interior courtyard

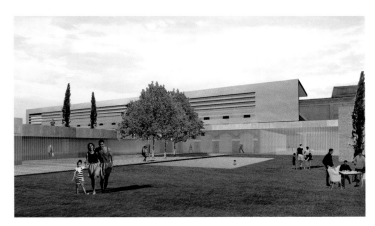

Rendered view of interior garden

Rendered view of living unit

Tennis Center

Madrid

The Spanish capital may have lost its bid for the 2012 Olympics, but Dominique Perrault's Tennis Center, originally slated as an Olympic venue and now being built for other tennis tournaments and special events, still captures the civic pride that large athletic facilities can bring to a city. Perrault's design for the site, which lies alongside the Manzanares River and contains a small lake, calls for a large box raised above the water on a series of stout columns, giving the complex the appearance of ever-so-slightly hovering aboveground. The building's presence is also subtly mirrored in the water it sits above.

Spectators reach the center by crossing a long footbridge that sits over the lake, bringing them to the ground level of the center, the facility's main hub. Athletes, the press, and staff are brought in through an entry on the opposite side. Inside, there are three stadiums, each with a different seating capacity. The main court dominates the interior volume; the other two courts inhabit the remainder, both sitting to its southern edge. The interstitial space between the three courts allows for circulation, concessions, and other functions. The exterior of the complex is clad in a metal mesh—characteristic of the architect's work—which allows the structure to be read as both a definitive rectangular volume and as a permeable, luminous screen.

The most striking feature of the complex is its roofing system. Each court has its own operable "lid" that can be mechanically pivoted upward. Most obviously, this allows the facility to operate during adverse weather by simply closing the lids. However, the system also allows the courts and their events to take on varying degrees, quite literally, of public display depending on how many of the lids are open and how far. If a stadium is lidded, the event within it remains quiet and unknown to the outside; if a lid is opened, audible traces of the activity will spill out of the box.

Perrault cleverly experiments with the stadium typology in several ways. First, he uses a subtractive strategy as his organizing principle, carving the stadiums out of a simple larger volume instead of explicitly articulating the rake of the seating or the circulation on the outside. Perrault also chooses to highlight components that are intangible, such as light, luminosity, and sound. Starting with something as simple as a box with a lid, the architect heightens the visitor's sensory experience while simultaneously crafting a new type of stadium.

—PC

Rendered view of entry ramp from north

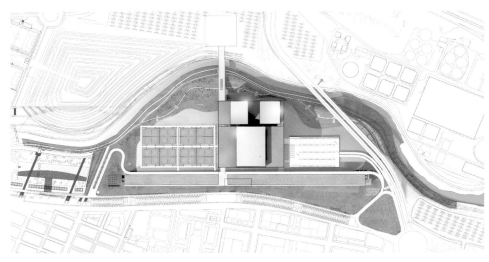

Site plan

Rendered view from north across the Manzanares River

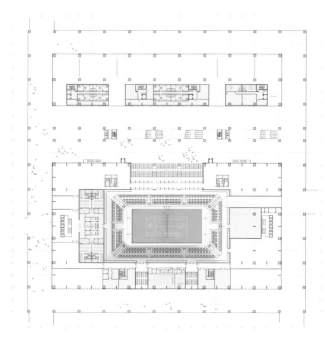

Plan, lower level

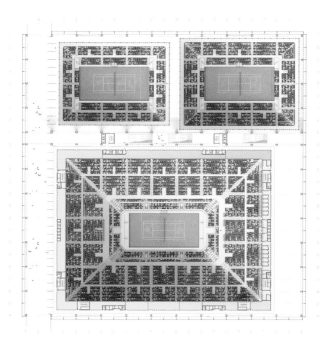

Plan, upper level

Rendered view of entry ramp from north, nighttime

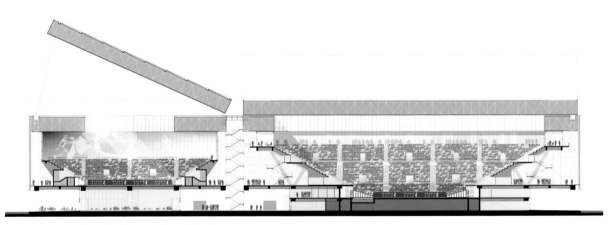

Transverse section through main court and grandstand court

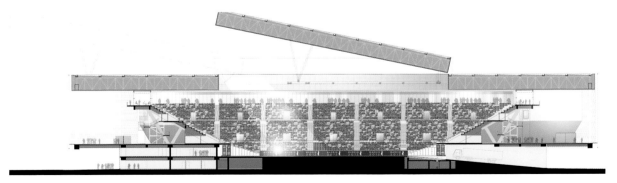

Longitudinal section through main court

Rendered view of main court

Model showing operable lids

Rendered view of main court converted into concert venue

Hotel at Marqués de Riscal Winery

Elciego, La Rioja

The Marqués de Riscal Winery in Elciego has enlisted Gehry Partners to create a singular destination for its winery and hotel facilities. Located in La Rioja, Spain's storied wine country, Marqués de Riscal is the oldest winery in the Basque country. The contemporary structure is prominently placed in this traditional setting, which includes two nineteenth-century sandstone buildings.

The main building, which will be the focal point of the vineyard's campus, houses a hotel, a restaurant, an exhibition space, and a reception area for wine-tasting. Several regular stone volumes emerge from the building's footprint, providing space for the structure's vertical circulation. The hotel rooms and other private spaces are elevated to the third, fourth, and fifth levels by these three "super-columns"—massive concrete pillars that support the loads of the upper stories. The floor slabs on these levels become increasingly small as they move upward, giving the internal volume a vaguely pyramidal shape.

The columns free up a tremendous amount of open space on the lower two levels, allowing the public areas to be largely free of partitions and affording panoramic vistas of the surrounding vineyard. A highly irregular wooden frame structure surrounds the building envelope and provides the skeleton upon which colored titanium ribbons rest. These ribbons form numerous undulating canopies, giving the building the fluid dynamism characteristic of Frank Gehry's work. On one side a footbridge emerges like a tail, connecting the building to a hotel extension on higher terrain.

The structurally innovative scheme marks a new notion of cultural tourism, bringing Gehry's signature work outside of the urban and suburban fabrics. Despite juxtaposing such a wholly contemporary language with the traditional rural context, the architects seem loath to compete with the surroundings. Instead, they allow both the sculpture and the setting to coexist and to serve equally as the attractions.

—PC

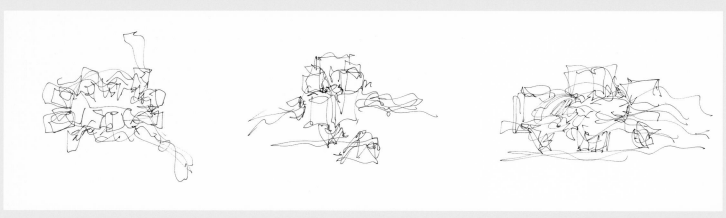

Sketches

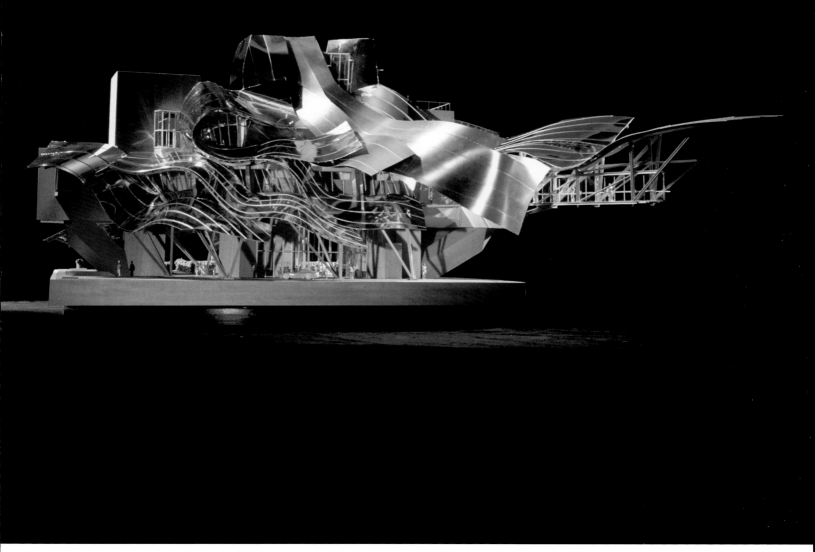

Model

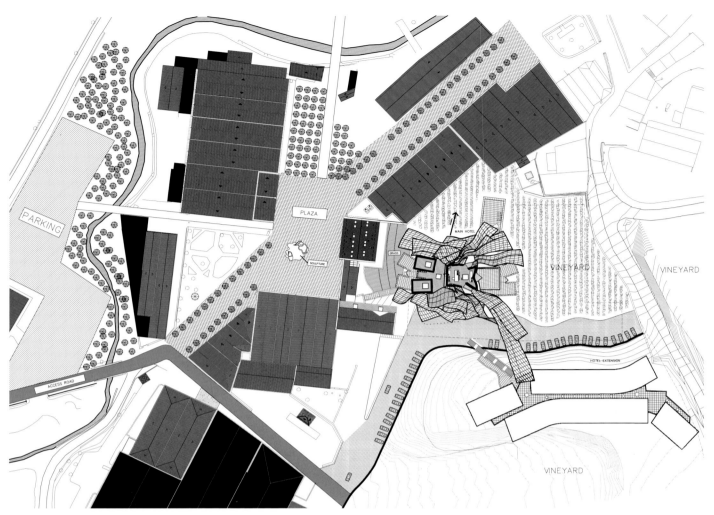

Site plan

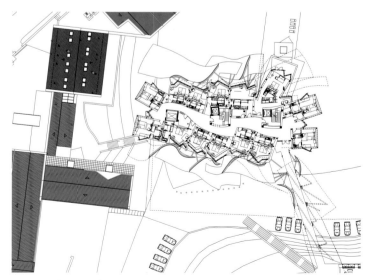

Plan, floor 3 (hotel level)

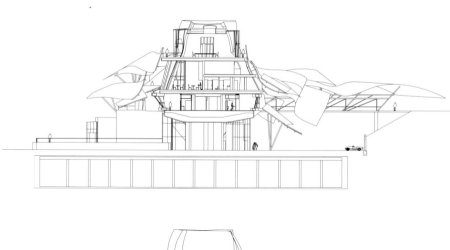

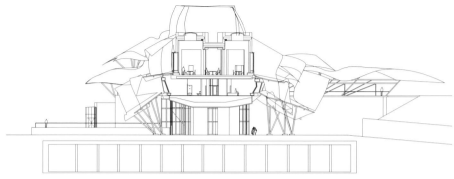

Transverse sections

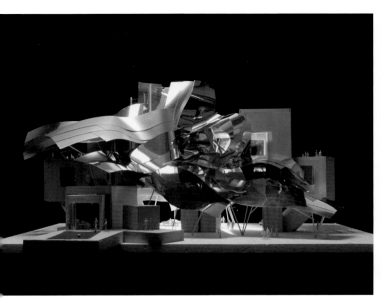

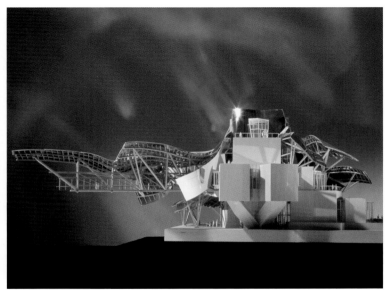

Models

Site panorama

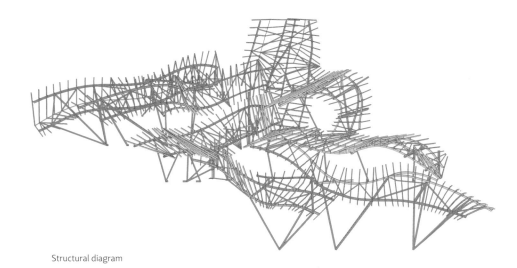
Structural diagram

Construction photos

Fuensanta Nieto and Enrique Sobejano   I   Nieto Sobejano Arquitectos

SE-30 Social Housing (2002)

Sevilla

Emilio Tuñón and Luis M. Mansilla | Mansilla+Tuñón, Arquitectos

Museum of Contemporary Art (MUSAC) (2005)

León

Health Center (2003)

Santa Eulalia, Ibiza

Urgències

Felipe Artengo Rufino, Fernando Martín Menis, and José M. Rodríguez-Pastrana Malagón with Mariola Merino Martín | AMP Arquitectos

Athletics Stadium

Santa Cruz de Tenerife

The Canary Islands lie a distant 828 miles southwest from Spain's mainland, near the western coast of Morocco. A volcanic archipelago, the seven islands are Spain's most tropical locale. Abounding with lush scenery, sandy beaches, and tremendous natural resources, the islands have enjoyed a prosperous tourist industry and marked population growth throughout the past century. This urban paradise is studded with reminders of its dramatic geological history, including massive rocks, lava flows, ravines, and craters. For their new regional athletics stadium in Santa Cruz de Tenerife, one of the islands' two capitals, the architects seek to camouflage the facility within the city's fabric as if it were just another geological phenomenon.

Located adjacent to a major vehicular roundabout, the stadium, consisting of a track and a field, is excavated out of the ground. The earth displaced by this subtractive strategy is butted to the track's perimeter, becoming an ellipsoidal rim and rendering the entire structure a craterlike indentation. This rim is further sculpted to create numerous vertical terraces that become the seating for over four thousand spectators. It is from these terraces that the enormous in situ transformation of the earth is most apparent. On the perimeter's long eastern edge, the rim is extruded toward the highway to create a convex embankment that houses administrative and auxiliary spaces as well as the ceremonial porticoed entry plaza.

The embankment is the site of the only additive architectural features of the stadium, a series of thirty-two tectonic concrete ribs. The ribs morph and elongate as they move from the sides toward the center, where the portico's overhang is the deepest. These concrete frames function as both post and lintel, supporting the horizontal load of the terraces as well as the vertical load of the awning and roof. Reminiscent of Rudolph Schindler's structural piers in his Lovell Beach House (1926), the graduated articulation of AMP's concrete piers is entirely dictated by the predetermined shape that these structures support. The embankment and rim are clad in rough excavated rock, obscuring the already minimal architectural intervention and offering a fitting finish to the building's primitive beauty.

—PC

Sketches

ABOVE: Rendered aerial view
OPPOSITE: Aerial rendering of track

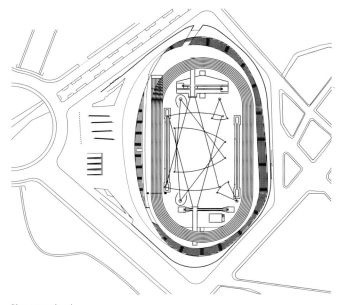

Plan, upper level

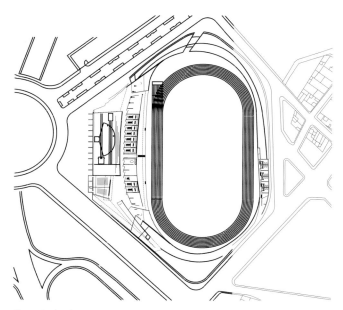

Plan, entry level

Sections through structural frames

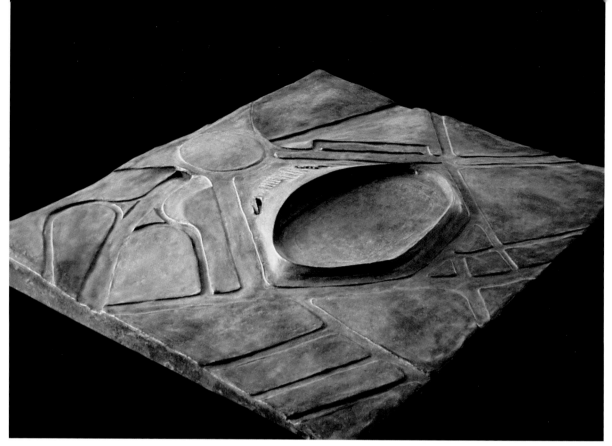

Model

Transverse section

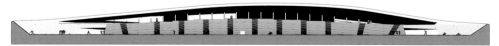

Longitudinal section through stadium

Transverse section through entry

Rendered view of entry plaza

Rendered view from southwest

Construction photo, structural frames

Construction photo, interior

Construction detail, exterior cladding

Rendered view of track

Eduardo Arroyo | NO.MAD Arquitectos

Casa Levene

San Lorenzo de El Escorial, Madrid

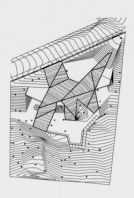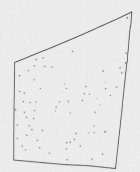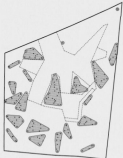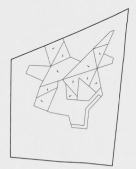

Site plan and diagrams showing site strategy

Eduardo Arroyo's Casa Levene is located on a wooded site in San Lorenzo de El Escorial, situated 3,200 feet above sea level and known for its panoramic views and sixteenth-century monastery. The private residence was designed to respect the preexisting forestation of the semiprotected setting, drawing upon natural processes and sensual engagement with the environment.

Rather than artificially clearing a site for the house, the faceted volume was derived by responding to and utilizing open areas amid clusters of trees. Studies were conducted to determine how the trees would filter the light and how shadows would be cast on each level of the house. The final form incorporates the slope of the site, the strict regulations on rooflines in this area, and the client's programmatic requirements.

The three levels, in which separate branches accommodate discrete functions, progress from public to private as they descend. The main entrance is on the third level. Two living areas, a game room, a bar, and an entertainment area are contained on this upper level. The middle level is occupied by a kitchen, dining area, covered outdoor terrace, and heated indoor pool. The lowest level contains the master bedroom, gym, and sauna. The house will feature varying levels of opacity and transparency to reflect different levels of contact with the exterior. Wood and amber resin on the interior will abstractly reflect the surrounding woods.

—TDC

Model, view from side

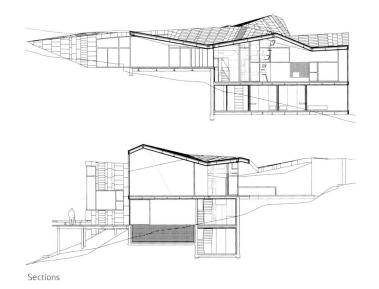

Sections

North elevation

Model, view from above

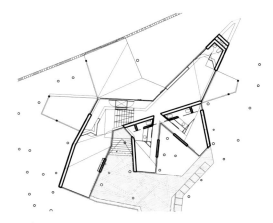

Plan, floor 2

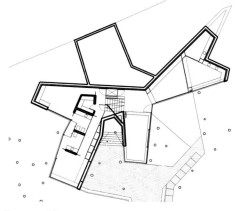

Plan, ground floor

Construction photo

Model, view from rear

IVAM Expansion

Valencia

The expansion of the Institut Valencià d'Art Modern serves dual purposes: to increase the museum's interior space and to magnify its presence within Valencia's old city. To accommodate a growing collection and the demand for more exhibition space, Kazuyo Sejima and Ryue Nishizawa have designed a large shell that fits loosely over IVAM's existing building, which was created in 1989 by Valencian architects Emilio Giménez and Carlos Salvadores. The original building is given over entirely to galleries while subsidiary functions, including a restaurant, auditorium, and offices, are pushed out and housed within the liminal space between the existing building and the new envelope.

The architects employ a perforated scrim of white-painted metal to define a new space that is both exterior and interior. The design process included careful studies of the skin's geometry as well as the angle, depth, position, and proportion of the punched holes, which allow natural light, wind, and precipitation to pass through and create a microclimate that the architects compare to "areas of filtered light under large trees." A mixture of fresh and climatized air tempers this environment. The grid of slender columns that supports the shell's roof forms a modern hypostyle hall that is at once of the city and within the museum's domain.

A terrace on the roof of the existing building grants vistas through the permeable skin out over Valencia's cityscape. There are two openings in the envelope's roof, which floats about 50 feet above the terrace. One, over the open-air restaurant, gives diners an unobstructed view up to the sky. The other is above the sculpture court, which is enclosed by walls and has no columns, creating an ambience discrete from the other terrace spaces. Here, an amorphous patch of smaller perforations runs along the roofline on the skin's south facade to protect the sculpture court against harsh sunlight.

Like a gauzy garment, IVAM's external skin generates gradations of transparency. During the day, the inner structure's shadowy form is discernible through the diaphanous shell. At night, when the museum is illuminated, the envelope becomes more transparent, exposing its contents to the city.

—AQ

ABOVE: Aerial site photo
OPPOSITE: Rendered view of main atrium

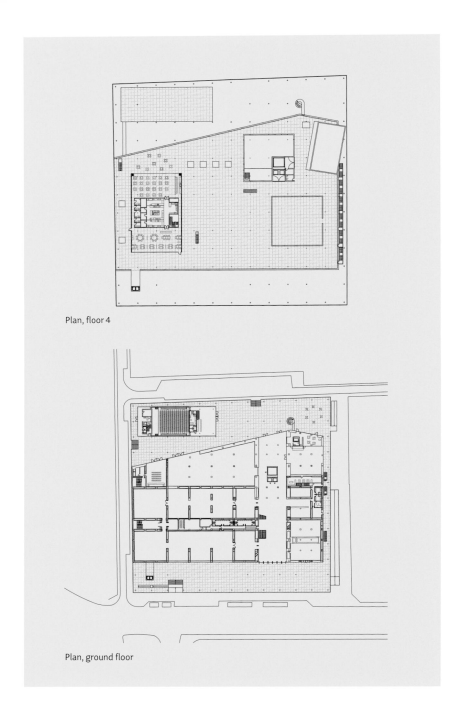

Plan, floor 4

Plan, ground floor

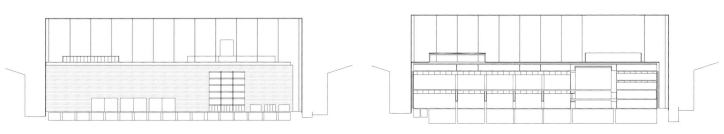

Section through east gallery

Section through central galleries

South elevation

West elevation

Rendered view, main atrium and Calle Guillem de Castro

Rendered view, upper galleries

Sharing Tower

Valencia

In 2003 Valencian architect Vicente Guallart organized a large-scale collaborative master plan for a housing development in Valencia. The focus was a campus of 2,500 new residential units whose aim is to rethink social-spatial relations, particularly among a range of lower- to middle-income groups. Originally situated on an 11-acre plot of land straddling an urban and rural setting, the site was later moved to an 86-acre footprint in the more urban La Torre district after the project was well received at the 2003 Valencia Biennial. Already existing on the site are four well-preserved farmhouses and several *huerta*, urban farms, that will remain intact. These farms, along with a new soccer field, track, and skating rink, are located roughly in the center of the site's footprint. Consequently, all housing lines the perimeter of the site, insulating the interior landscape. This perimeter is parceled into sixteen plots for sixteen different architects. Each architect must provide their share of housing units along with spaces for education, cultural activities, and artists' studios. Among the other participants are Abalos&Herreros, Eduardo Arroyo, José María Torres Nadal, Toyo Ito, MVRDV, Greg Lynn FORM, and Josep Lluís Mateo – MAP Arquitectos.

Guallart began his investigation for his own plot by examining the needs of different demographic groups, including immigrants, students, families, the disabled, and the elderly. Exhaustively charting patterns in lifestyle and consumption, Guallart's research calls for maximizing the use of resources such as televisions, laundry facilities, and computers by sharing them among like-minded tenants.

The building, aptly titled Sharing Tower, rises sixteen stories above its lower parking level. The tower appears to be a striated stack of "discs," each with a central core that will house common space. These cores consist of widened corridors that take on a variety of configurations as they split or diverge, always terminating at the glazed perimeter in order to provide ample natural light for the interior areas. The tower's stairs and elevators are pushed to the perimeter, emphasizing that the core be a meeting place and not a circulation route. The private spaces, for sleeping, showering, dressing, and so on, are then nestled into the remaining areas; while basic in their accommodations, they provide panoramic ribbon-windows with uninterrupted views of the Valencian countryside. Adjacent to the

tower, the building has arms that hug a central courtyard, which is intended for the staging of urban events, such as concerts and performances. These arms—one of which is elevated three stories above ground to open the courtyard onto the greater site—house the complex's other programs, including schools, shopping, and a theater.

Recalling the 1927 Weissenhof project in Stuttgart, Guallart's master plan brings together a diverse group of architects and functions as an experiment in transposing contemporary lifestyles into new approaches in mass housing. Sharing Tower is an ambitious testament to that legacy, updated and adapted for use in modern-day Spain.

—PC

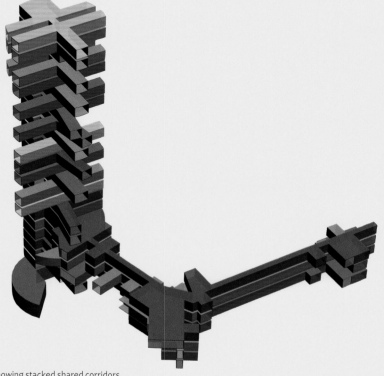

Axonometric showing stacked shared corridors

Rendered view of tower and public plaza

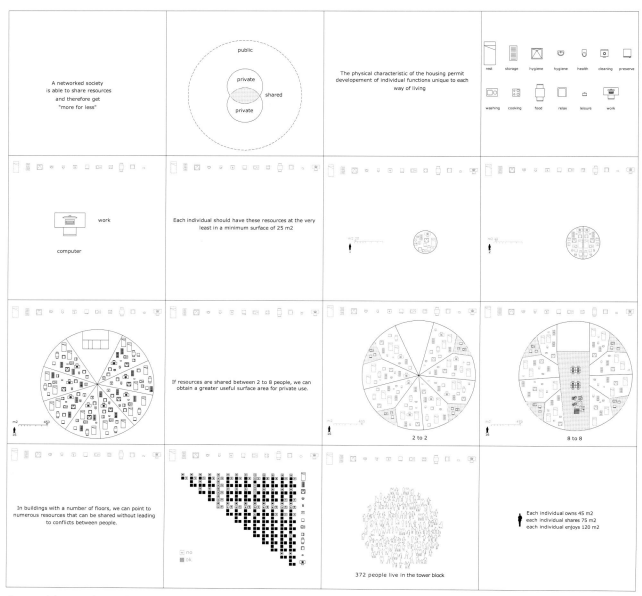

A networked society
is able to share resources
and therefore get
"more for less"

public
private
shared
private

The physical characteristic of the housing permit
developement of individual functions unique to each
way of living

rest storage hygiene hygiene health cleaning preserve

washing cooking food relax leisure work

work

computer

Each individual should have these resources at the very
least in a minimum surface of 25 m2

If resources are shared between 2 to 8 people, we can
obtain a greater useful surface area for private use.

2 to 2

8 to 8

In buildings with a number of floors, we can point to
numerous resources that can be shared without leading
to conflicts between people.

no
ok

372 people live in the tower block

Each individual owns 45 m2
each individual shares 75 m2
each individual enjoys 120 m2

Conceptual diagrams showing sharing strategies

Interior rendering of private units

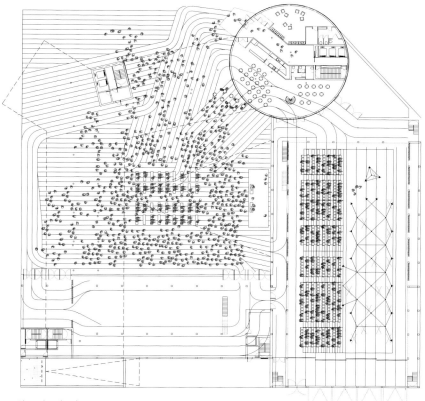

Plan, plaza level

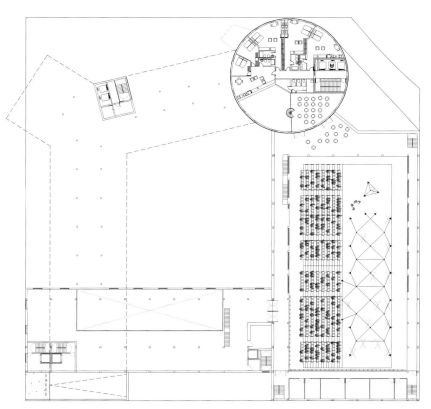

Plan, auditorium level

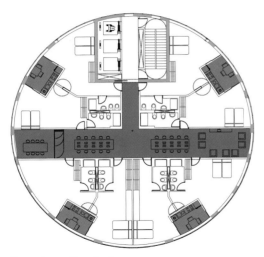

Tower plan, configuration 3

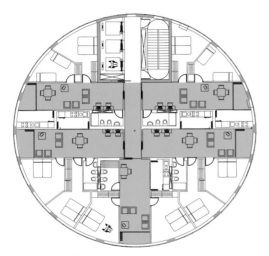

Tower plan, configuration 2

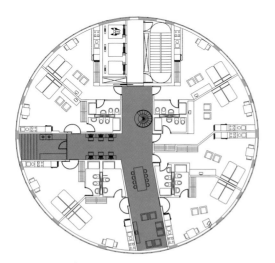

Tower plan, configuration 1

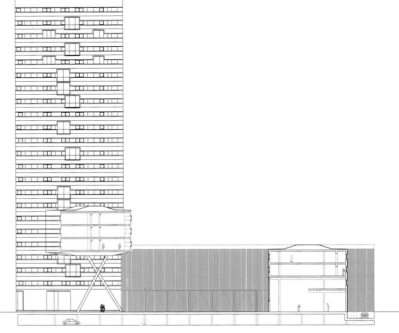

East–west section

Interior renderings of shared corridor

Guillermo Vázquez Consuegra

National Museum of Marine Archaeology

Cartagena, Murcia

Cartagena, a Mediterranean port founded by the Carthaginians and long an important naval base for Spain, is rich with archaeological sites. The city has initiated a revitalization of the wharf platform constructed along the waterfront in the nineteenth century, which until recently was relegated to industrial use. In his project for the National Museum of Marine Archaeology, situated within this built-up wharf, Guillermo Vázquez Consuegra draws from Cartagena's physical and historical context.

Positioned between a new traffic thoroughfare and the seafront, the museum links more dynamic urban developments to the derelict wharf. The building's program is divided between two discrete elements: a linear volume, which houses a marine research center, and a jagged form, which contains public exhibition spaces. These two parallel volumes define outdoor spaces, including a plaza and an open-air vestibule, that form the public face of the museum. The constructions emerge above the wharf's surface like giant light wells that illuminate the excavated building below. The museum's subterranean development is due to limitations imposed by the city on the buildable area of the wharf, but also to the architect's desire to echo the underwater theme of the building's program.

The research facility is a slender rectangular volume clad in sand-colored concrete and zinc panels. Its private and semi-public spaces are organized on three levels: two above ground and one below. Angled skylights on the roof bring light and ventilation into double-height workspaces, and on the south facade a clerestory slices the building's mass where it meets the ground, admitting light to the lower level.

The aboveground presence of the exhibition galleries is an irregular steel and zinc-louvered glass construction that introduces natural light to the exhibition spaces while allowing views down into the interior from the public plaza of the wharf. The vitreous structure covers the permanent exhibition gallery, a 46-foot-high space in which boats and other large objects may be displayed and even suspended from the ceiling.

To enter the museum visitors must pass between the two volumes and down a ramp leading below the wharf's surface to an entry space at the western extreme of the building that allows dramatic views down the length of the excavated floor plate. From here, one can access an underground link to the research center building as well as

exhibition spaces, activities workshops, an auditorium, and a restaurant on staggered platforms within the carved-out building. A space for temporary exhibitions extends to the wharf's edge, where a large window frames views of the sea.

Embodying Gottfried Semper's notion of opposition between a lightweight tectonic structure perched above a massive stereotomic earthwork, the project provides unusual sectional variety. The buried building permits the development of large open civic spaces at the wharf's surface while its aboveground projections command a striking presence within the incipient harbor development.

—AQ

Sketch

Model, view from west

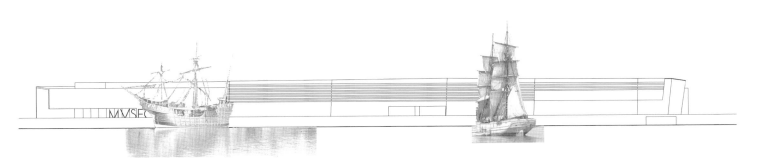

South elevation

Sketch

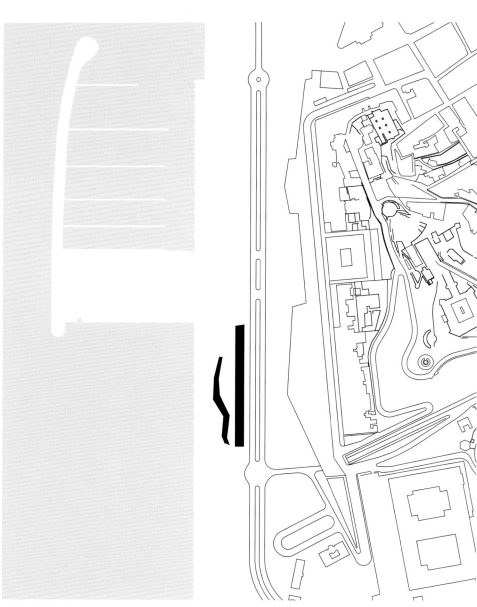

Site plan

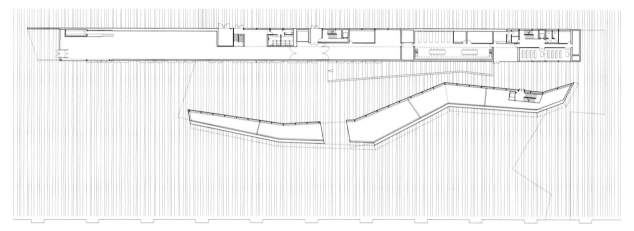

Plan, first floor

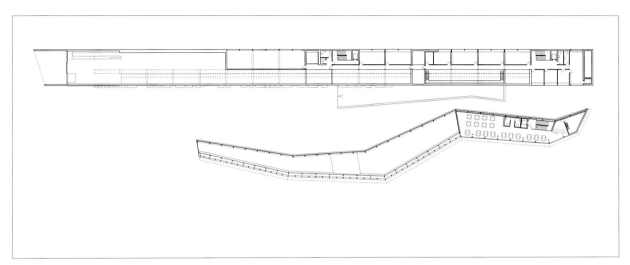

Plan, ground floor

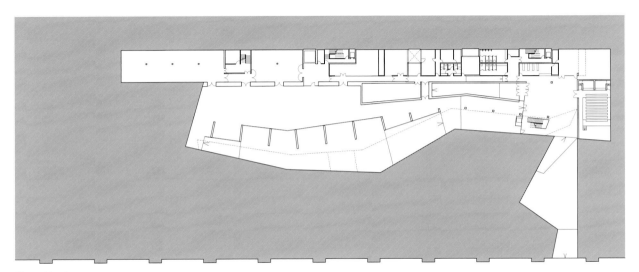

Plan, sublevel

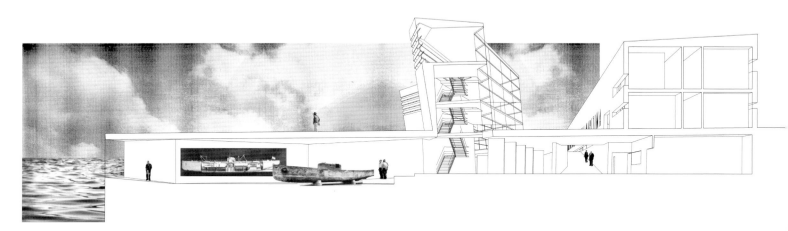

Transverse sectional perspective looking east

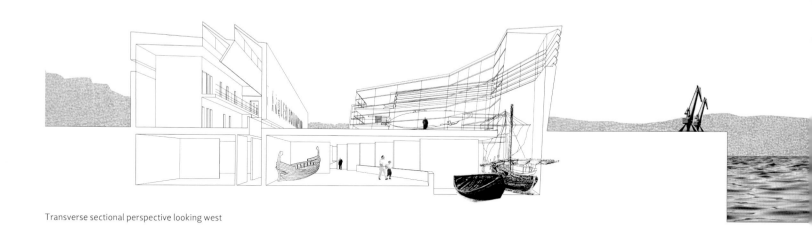

Transverse sectional perspective looking west

Longitudinal section through underground connection

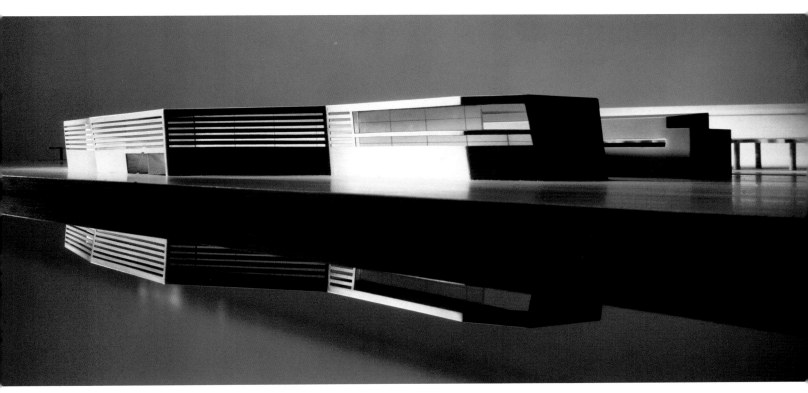

Model, view from east

La Ciudad del Flamenco

Jerez de la Frontera, Cádiz

Jerez de la Frontera, in the southwest of Andalucía, is considered the cradle of flamenco music and dance in Spain. Flamenco, born of a mosaic of Arab, Jewish, and Gypsy peoples with Persian and Roman influences, is the arresting pulse of the city. Swiss architects Jacques Herzog and Pierre de Meuron's winning competition scheme takes inspiration from this hybrid to create La Ciudad del Flamenco. With the goal of promoting contemporary flamenco culture, the architects have envisioned a complex—including an auditorium, a dance school, a research center, and a museum—that draws on architectural cues such as traditional Arab and Gypsy ornamentation and Andalusian courtyards.

The project encloses Plaza Belén, a neglected public square located in Jerez's city center, revitalizing this shady space while leaving the existing trees and overgrown shrubbery largely intact. The plaza's perimeter is built up as a two-story inhabitable wall that houses the complex's varied programs. From nearly every vantage within the complex one has a view onto the central courtyard. Anchoring the complex's southeast corner is the museum. Like a minaret, this tower acts as a beacon for tourists and flamenco enthusiasts alike, simultaneously referencing important local landmarks like the Alcázar and the Jerez Cathedral. Up close, the seemingly solid facade gives way to a delicately patterned screen, derived from the traditional Arab and Gypsy ornament. This screen functions not only as the building's textured skin but also becomes a perforated wall that, by nightfall, emanates light, transforming from a fortress to a living, glowing lamp.

As the seat of a highly traditional and indigenous musical culture, Jerez itself is an outdoor museum. The architects, in creating a vibrant, living treasury of flamenco that blends seamlessly with the city, formalize that idea with characteristic virtuosity, confirming the art form's significance while ensuring its posterity.

—PC

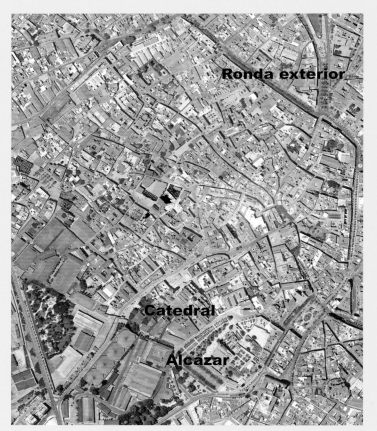

Site plan

Rendered view of exterior from west

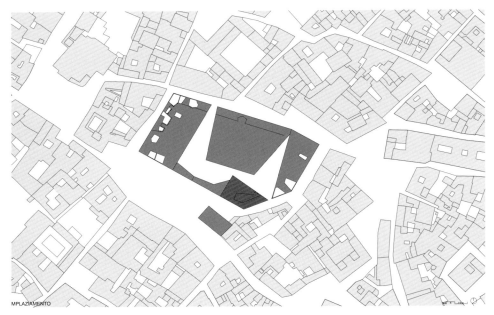

MPLAZIAMENTO

Plan, plaza and complex

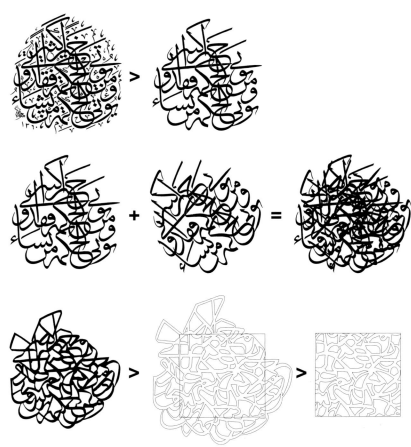

Diagram of facade derivation

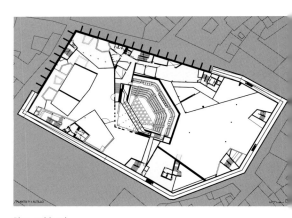

PLANTA P-1 ALTILLO

Plan, sublevel

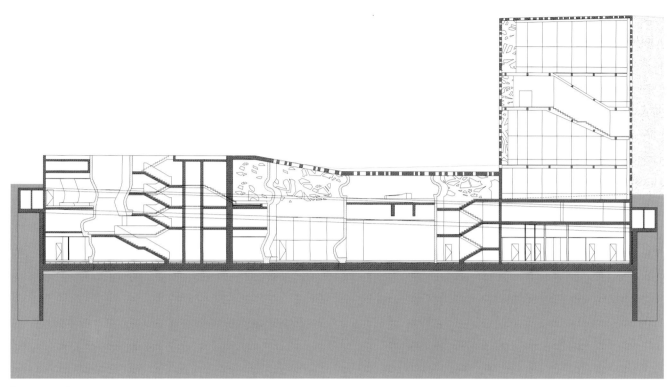

East–west section

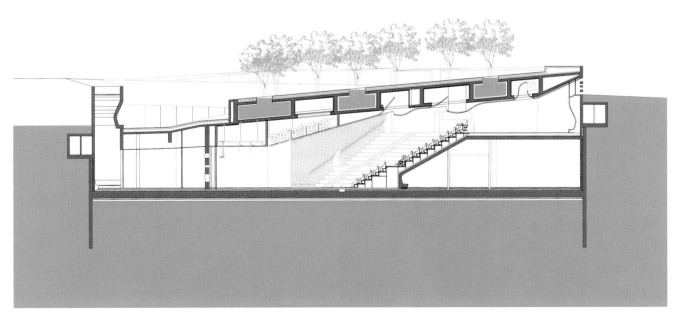

North–south section through auditorium

Rendered view of courtyard

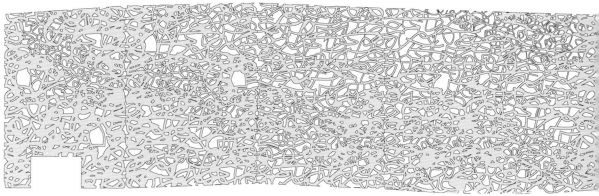

Diagram of facade foldout

Rendered view of main lobby

Rendered view of museum

Rendered view of auditorium

Bioclimatic Towers

Vitoria-Gastéiz

The Bioclimatic Towers, a complex of mixed-use buildings currently being built in Vitoria-Gastéiz, are positioned at the frontier of the expanding Salburúa district, where the city meets low-lying wetlands. The project, designed by Iñaki Ábalos, Juan Herreros, and Renata Sentkiewicz, consists of four simple rectangular towers strung along a curved road that serves as the limit between the extended urban ground and the marshland beyond. The first five levels of each building are given over to commercial and office space, while residential apartments at the upper levels have elevated perspectives over the surrounding landscape.

Each tower is rotated to maximize views over the fenland and to take advantage of optimal solar orientations. The dynamic composition of volumes ensures that as one circumnavigates the site the towers are not all viewed from the same angle, thus imparting a more slender appearance to the cluster of buildings. In addition, the shallow man-made lake at the base of the towers forms a mirrored surface that duplicates the structures, elongating their forms. This "liquid garden" also cools the public spaces surrounding the towers and blends the urban expansion with the surrounding swampy habitat.

The project's bioclimatic strategy involves various means of harnessing and storing solar energy. The architects carried out detailed studies of solar heating on the towers' facades before sizing and placing the bioclimatic components to ensure that each apartment and office space would achieve thermal comfort. Each facade incorporates opaque, translucent, and transparent panels composed of corrugated polycarbonate over cork, polycarbonate over glass, and transparent glass, respectively. Solar panels mounted to windows on the towers' central stair cores collect solar energy, which is then stored by accumulators at the basement level and later used to heat and cool the buildings' water supply. The opaque portions of the facades will act as Trombe walls that absorb thermal energy during the day, store it, and then release the energy to heat the buildings throughout the night. Heated concrete floor decks distribute heat evenly throughout interior spaces. Ventilated facades in the office areas and solar flues or conduits connected to the accumulators serve to increase air circulation and cool the buildings in hot weather.

The Bioclimatic Towers provide a model for how to build within the rapidly expanding urban periphery currently observed throughout much of Spain and Europe. The project's formal composition generates a distinctive icon within a largely homogenous urban fabric, and its use of passive strategies to achieve greater energy efficiency offers an example of sustainable construction within accelerated urban development.

—AQ

ABOVE: Site plan
OPPOSITE: Model, aerial view from north

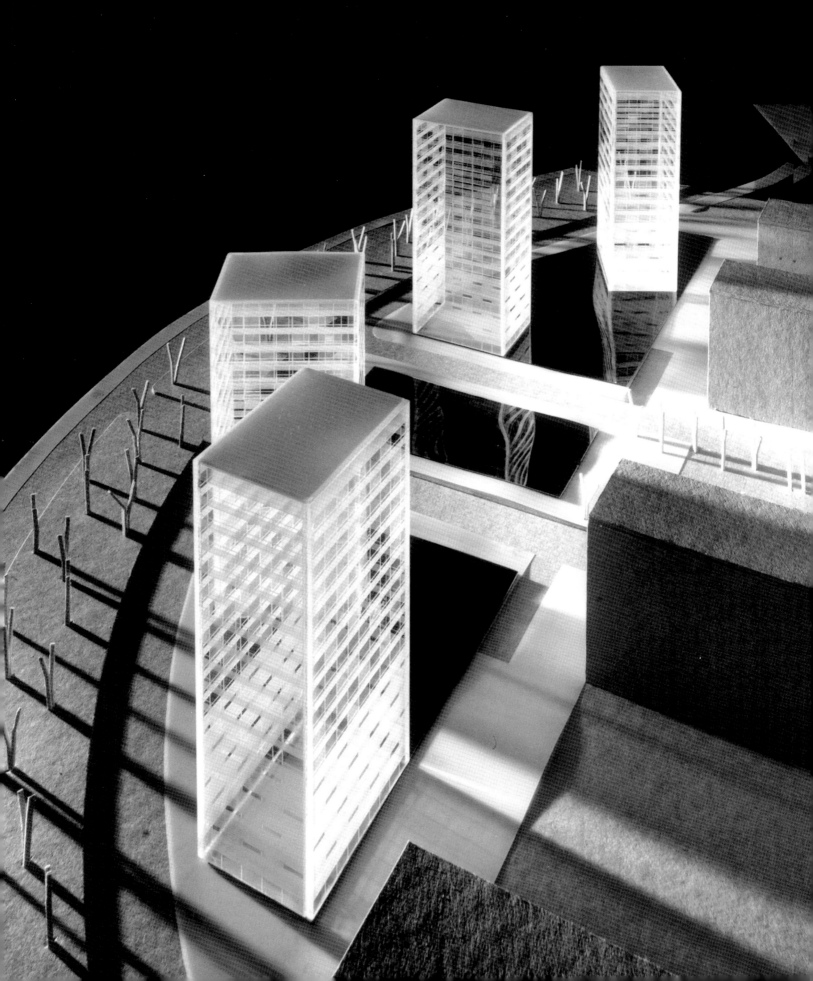

Model, view from east

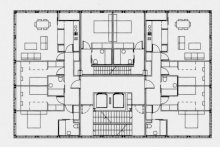

LEFT TO RIGHT: Typical plans, towers 1–4

Longitudinal section

Elevation detail

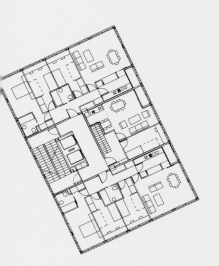

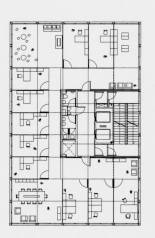

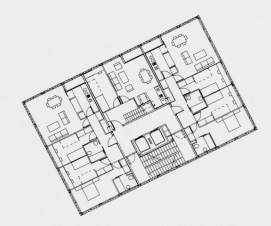

East elevation

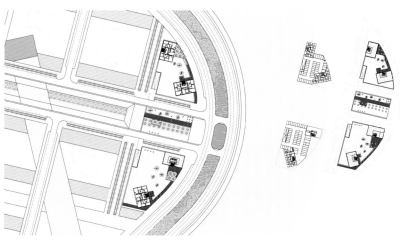

Site plan detail

Construction photo

Barcelona

Enric Miralles and Benedetta Tagliabue | EMBT Miralles Tagliabue
Arquitectes Associats

Santa Caterina Market (2005)

Access to the Paseo del Ovalo (2004)

Teruel

Rafael Moneo

Town Hall Extension (1998)

Murcia

Centro de Talasoterapia

Gijón

Francisco Leiva Ivorra and grupo aranea's Centro de Talasoterapia, a low-lying complex that includes a spa, a hotel, and public space, is located at the edge of the sea in Gijón in the northwest of Spain. Thalassotherapy—seawater treatments believed to aid with stress, aging, hypertension, and arthritis, among other ills—was founded by Frenchman Louison Boubet in Brittany and gained popularity in the 1960s. This center will be one of the few located in Spain.

The building was designed to engage with its surroundings and to create a renewed sense of community while retaining its own formal autonomy. To achieve this, the architects conceived of the center as a partially eroded stone swept in from the sea, its loosely ovoid form open to the water. Public footpaths in the form of ramps and stairs, which appear to be a seamless continuation of the beach, cross the center. The peripheral walls contain the spa and hotel. The division of program responds to three different levels of publicness. The spa areas, which can be accessed either directly from the plaza or from the hotel, are the most secluded. Cocooned in the interior narrow zones of the building, they range from completely private treatment rooms to shared bathing areas—top-lit spaces designed to maximize the senses of sight, touch, smell, sound, and taste. By contrast, the five-star hotel fronts the sea. Sixty differentiated rooms with terraces give out onto the open expanse, allowing the visitor to relax and contemplate the infinite vista. The footpaths continue the maritime walk through the spa and hotel without disrupting the privacy of the guests, and conclude by encountering cafeterias, restaurants, and amenities for public use.

—TDC

Aerial rendering of Gijón from southeast

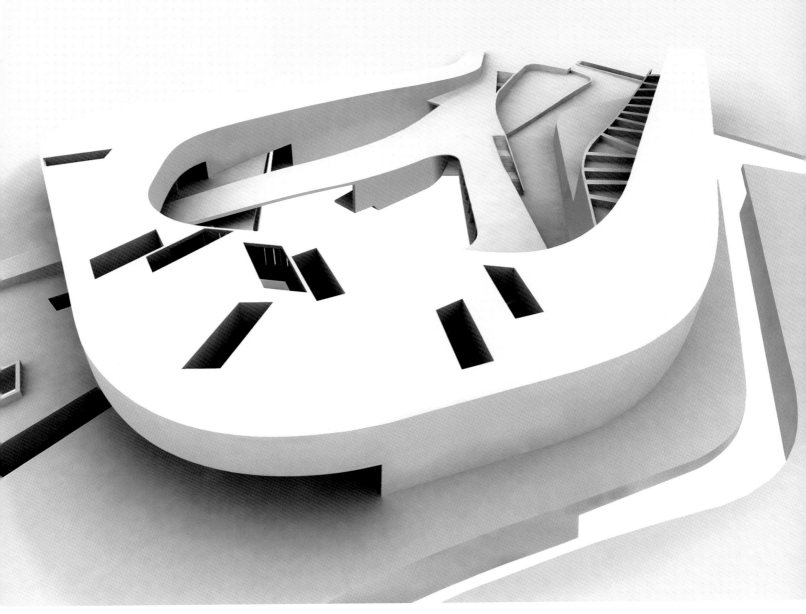

Aerial rendering from southwest

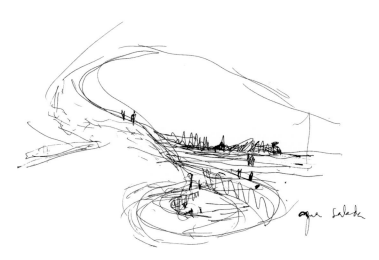

Sketch

Plan, floor 2

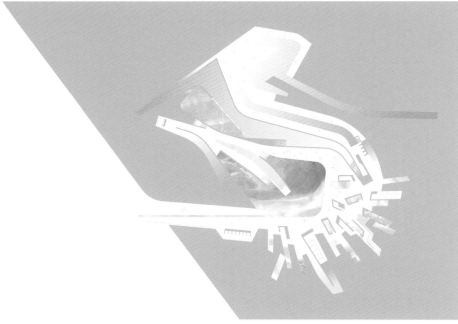

Plan, pool level, ground floor

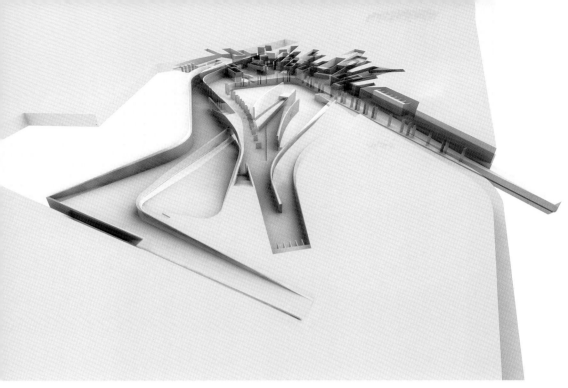

Aerial rendering from northeast showing interior divisions

Rendered view of interior pool

Transverse section

Longitudinal section

Rendered view from west

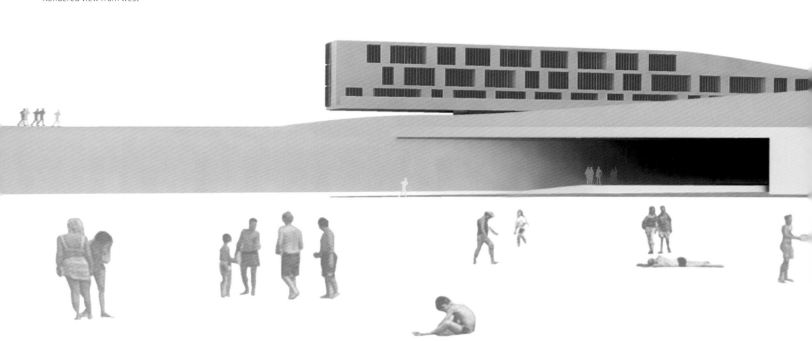

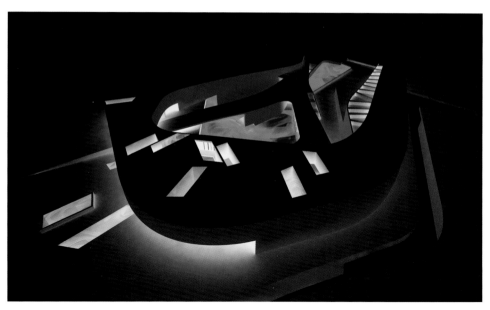

Aerial rendering from south, nighttime

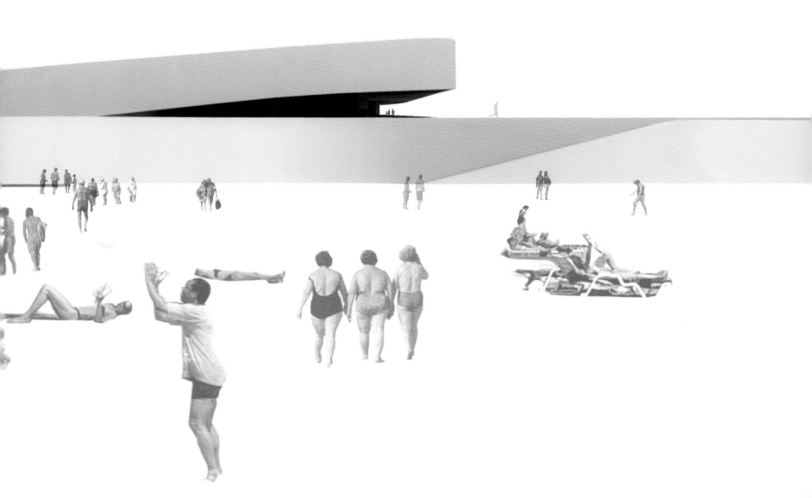

Housing Tower

Valencia

Josep Lluís Mateo's housing tower on the outskirts of Valencia occupies that margin common in expanding cities, where urban development meets open fields. The grass-covered parking lot at the foot of the building forms an uninterrupted horizontal green base that links the structure to the surrounding countryside. The tower itself is elevated one level above ground; its minimal footprint reduces the amount of impermeable ground-cover required and allows the landscape to extend beneath the building.

The tower is supported by four external and three internal concrete walls. The internal walls, one running the length of the floor plate and two others in the transverse direction, act as diaphragms that divide the interior spaces into six vertical tubes. Within these tubes, modules are arranged in various configurations to create apartments of differing dimensions that are distributed throughout the twenty floors of the tower. In contrast, the four external walls are treated as great vertical beams on which one may map the trajectory of forces in a type of full-scale stress diagram. A subtraction operation is employed to remove material from areas of this concrete armature that are not required to carry forces, so that a "structural fabric" emerges in which the arc of unloading can be read in the irregular grid of perforations. The exterior walls thus act as both structure and enclosure; the more solid portions express points of greater load. The building's facades will be left as bare polished concrete, giving the structure a stark presence.

The otherwise regular orthogonal volume of the tower has been altered at three points: at the ground its footprint is reduced to preserve green space; in its midsection a void is carved out to house an elevated garden; and at its roofline another void creates space for solar panels and a cistern to collect rainwater. Throughout the project, Mateo endeavors to decrease the environmental impact of the building using passive strategies, from siting to exploit prevailing breezes and natural light to selecting materials that have a minimum environmental impact throughout their life cycles.

—AQ

Site plan

Rendered view from highway

Plan, floors 1 and 2

Plan, floor 6

Plan, floors 8–16

Plan, floors 17 and 19

Plan, floors 18 and 20

Transverse section

Transverse section

Longitudinal section

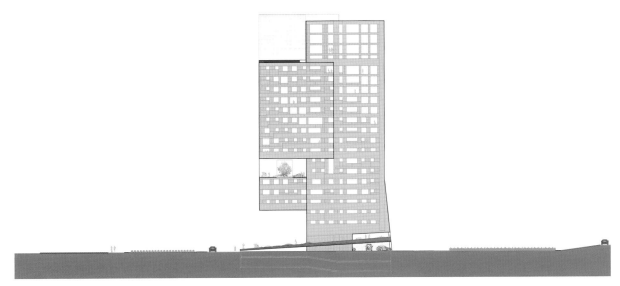

West elevation

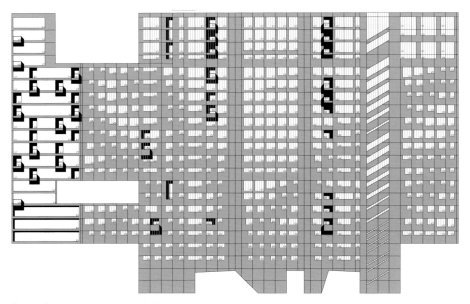

Facade diagram showing structural scheme

Rendered view from south

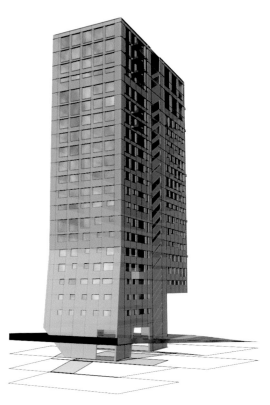

Rendered view from north

Rendered view from southeast

Congress Center

Córdoba

Rem Koolhaas and Ellen van Loon's Congress Center is an elongated building situated across the river from Córdoba's medieval heart. Its linear form maximizes vantages toward the Alcázar, the Great Mosque, and the historic center while creating a boundary for the modern city. The building is sited at 90 degrees to a public plaza. A wedge-shaped volume, which juts out from the eastern end of the south facade and houses the center's main auditorium, serves as an entrance canopy. Supported on massive angled columns, it establishes a strong presence on the street and visually and spatially connects the structure to the adjacent plaza.

A public, open-air promenade runs through the center of the building, forming an elevated pedestrian street. This main axis is punctuated by two cores of vertical circulation. The solid area that surrounds the promenade is dedicated to meeting areas and hotel rooms above and to convention areas and the hotel lobby below. Secondary systems of escalators and stairs provide access from the promenade to areas above and below. The promenade widens where it intersects the main auditorium, as if being pried open. This widening creates a large, open expanse behind the shallow stage—used primarily for conferences—through which the spectator can see out to the city and the pedestrian can see into the auditorium. Flanking the auditorium are an open-air cinema to the west and a smaller theater to the east.

The design hinges on solid and void spaces that correspond to the building's private and public programs, respectively. The concrete structure is clad with three different types of manipulated glass planks—irregularly patterned green, smooth green, and clear—that create varying levels of transparency corresponding to the center's programmatic offerings. A regular columnar grid provides the structure on the eastern end. As the building progresses toward the west, a system of trusses complements and gradually replaces the columns, allowing for large open expanses in the foyer, main auditorium, and theater.

—TDC

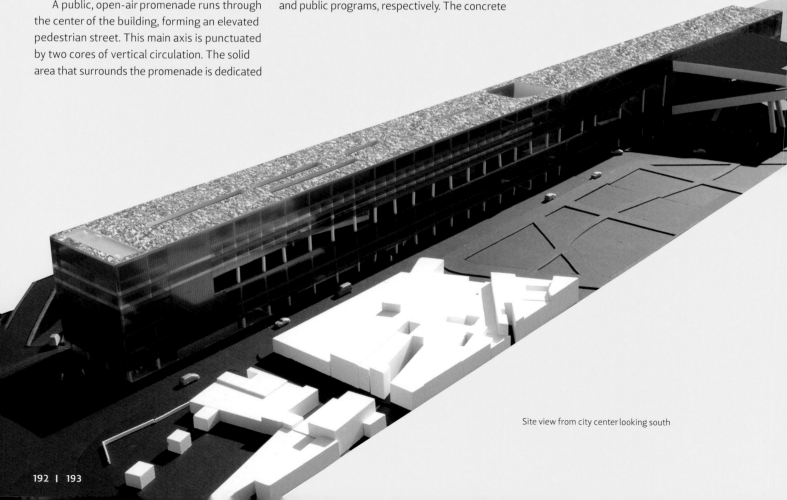

Site view from city center looking south

Rendered site view from southeast across Guadalquivir River, showing historic city center

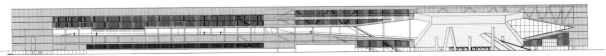

South elevation

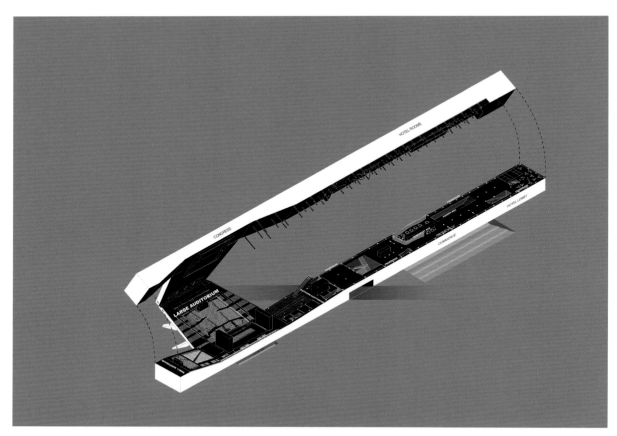

Programmatic and structural diagram

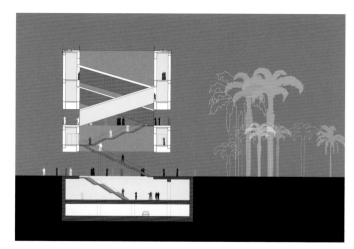

Transverse section through atrium

Transverse section through hotel

Model detail showing main auditorium and entry

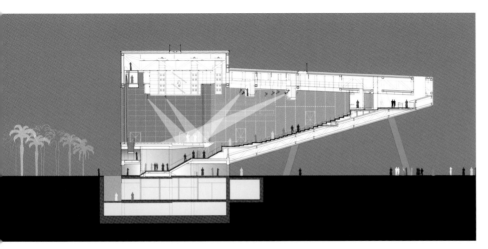

Transverse section through main auditorium

Facade material studies

Model, facade detail

Model, view from west showing roofscape and elevated public promenade

Rendered view, lobby toward indoor auditorium

Rendered view, outdoor auditorium

Performing Arts Center

Vitoria-Gastéiz

Juan Navarro Baldeweg's Performing Arts Center lies just outside the medieval center of the small Basque town of Vitoria-Gastéiz. Its asymmetrical six-sided volume reflects the irregularity of the historic city plan while creating views toward surrounding gardens and trees. A highly gestural canopy drapes over the folded volume on four sides, bowing to the scale of a nearby church.

The center houses two venues for music: a fan-shaped symphonic auditorium and a smaller square hall for chamber music. The two-tiered auditorium is located directly off the entry and the more intimate hall is situated directly to the right. The residual area between the two spaces and the six-sided shell functions as circulation, with passageways, stairs, and foyers.

The center was inspired by what the architect considers the dual nature of the theater, that of being both a mysterious black box and a metaphoric open door. The saturated tones of blue, green, and red and the calligraphic improvisation of the canopy—a strong contrast to the monochromatic and highly geometrized shell—is a clear reference to the influence of Henri Matisse and Willem de Kooning. Baldeweg's use of light and color reflects not only his admiration of painterly abstraction but his belief that these elements are essential to our physical environment and individual natures.

—TDC

Model, entry detail

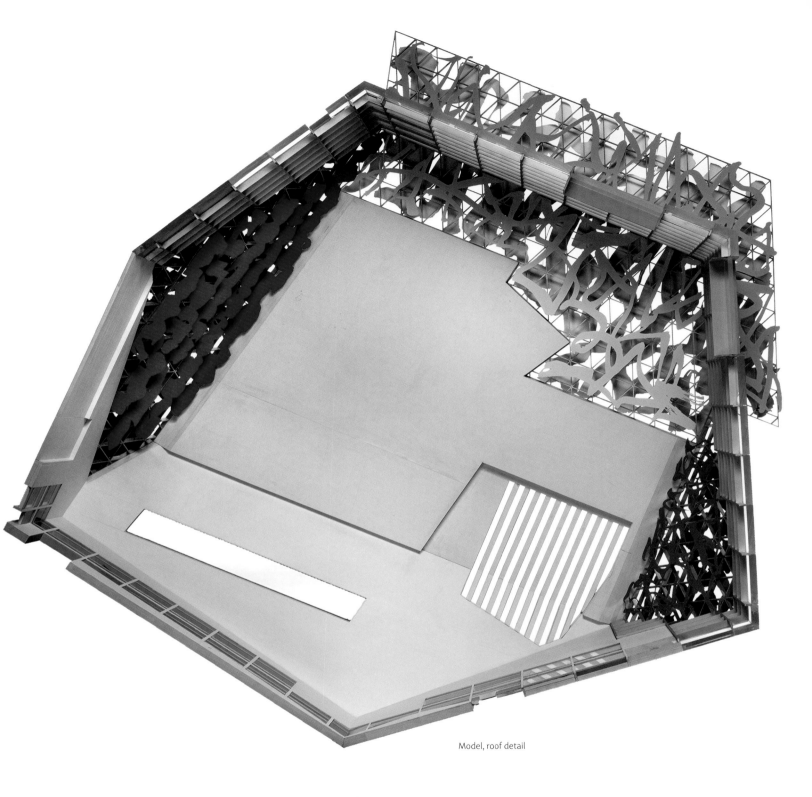

Model, roof detail

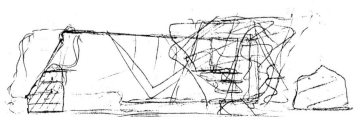

Sketch

Site plan

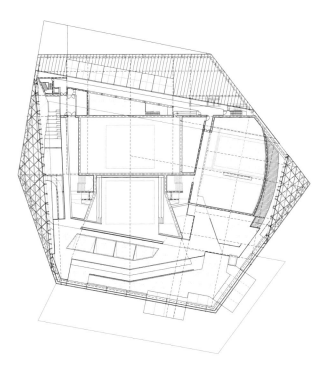

Plan, upper office level

Model, rear view

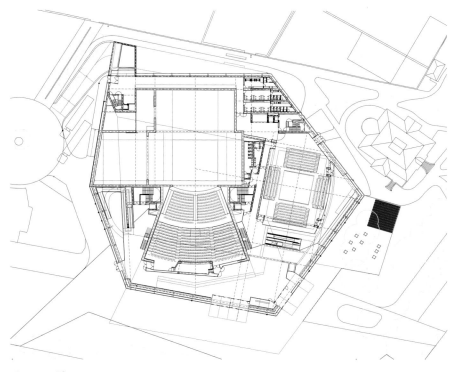

Plan, ground floor

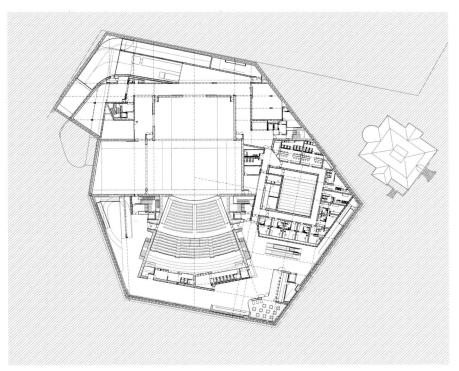

Plan, sublevel

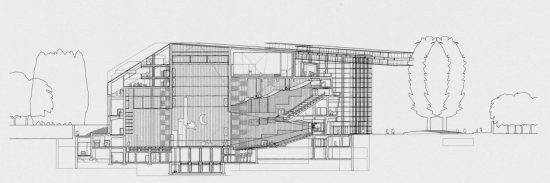

North–south section

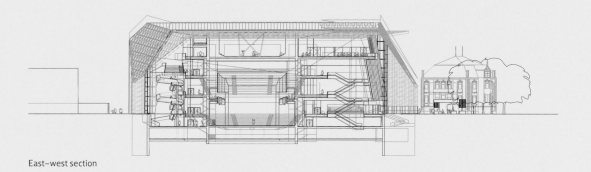

East–west section

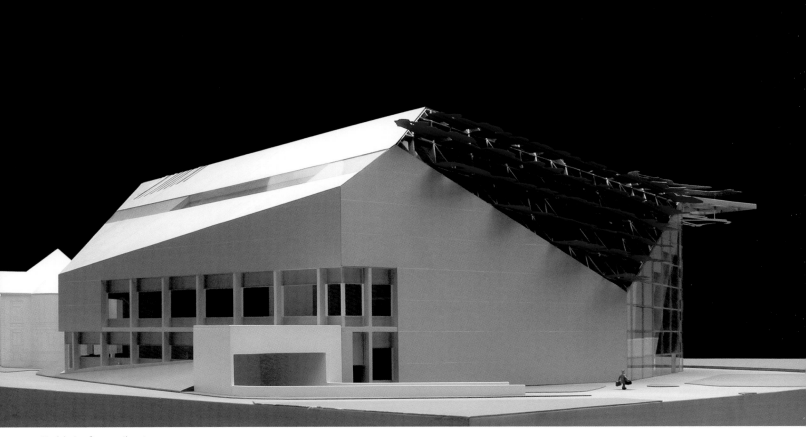

Model, view from northeast

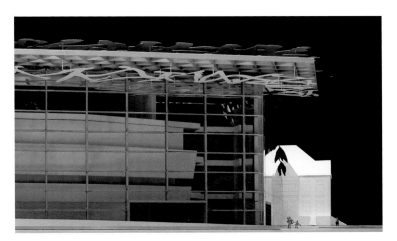

Model, facade detail

José Maria Torres Nadal + Antonio Marquerie

Theater and Auditorium

La Vila Joiosa, Alicante

La Vila Joiosa is a small tourist town located in southeastern Spain. Mount Puig Campana forms its scenic backdrop. José Maria Torres Nadal and Antonio Marquerie's Theater and Auditorium was designed to minimize the visual impact on this setting but still provide ample public space. The project's program for a 800-seat theater and auditorium, a 70-seat choir hall used for rehearsals and auditions, conference rooms, rehearsal rooms, and administrative offices is spread over a corner site and housed within a spiral form, which appears as if it is unraveling from center to periphery.

The ground floor of the main volume houses two conference rooms, which together can hold up to two hundred people. The auditorium is located on the next level; the choir hall is on the top level, suspended above the main hall and visible from below. The exterior volume—what the architects consider a circular arm and which contains rehearsal and administrative spaces—is elevated above the ground and loosely wraps the auditorium, creating an open plaza in the center. This raised threshold helps to mediate between the city and auditorium. The plaza, often swathed in strong shadows, becomes a public stage, providing an outdoor space for informal gathering. Upon entering the main interior volume, one proceeds through a hall either to the conference rooms or to a stair that leads to the foyer on the first level. From the foyer one can proceed either to the auditorium or to the secondary spaces in the arm.

The interiors of both halls have red linoleum floors, red seats, gray concrete walls, and a white polycarbonate faceted ceiling. Acoustics are designed for a variety of uses, including musical performances, conferences, and lectures. A bar acts as a transitional space between the foyer and the secondary spaces of the circular arm.

—TDC

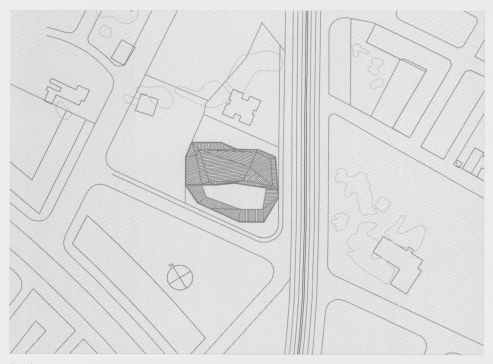

Site plan

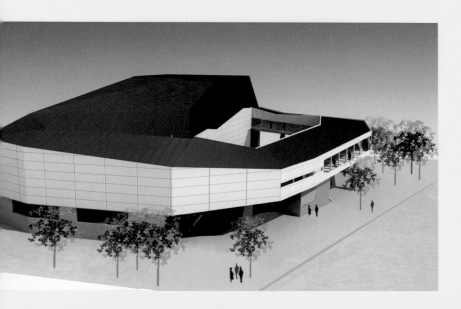

Rendered views of building perimeter

Rendered views toward plaza

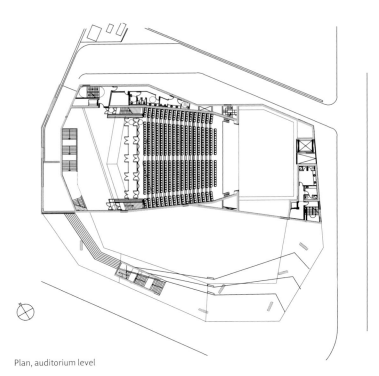

Plan, auditorium level

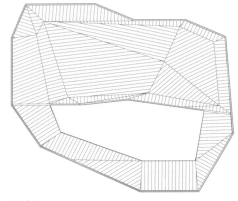

Roof plan

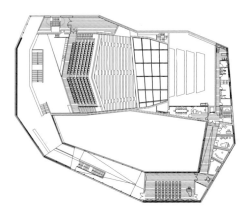

Plan, upper administrative level

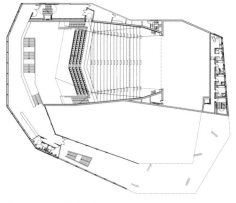

Plan, upper auditorium level

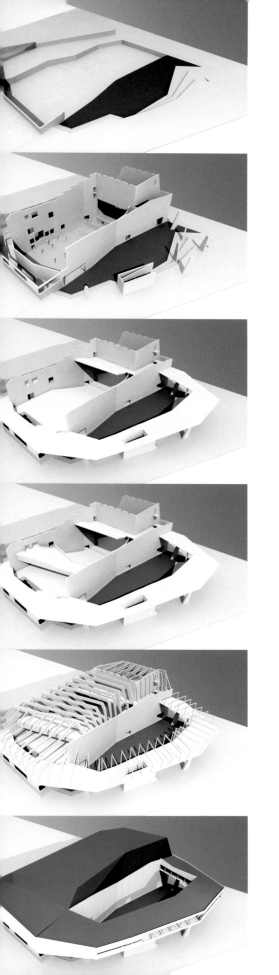

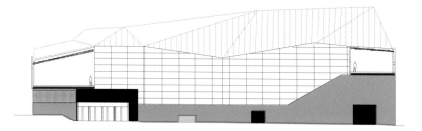

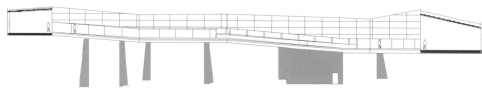

Sectional elevations from interior courtyard

Computer models showing structural development

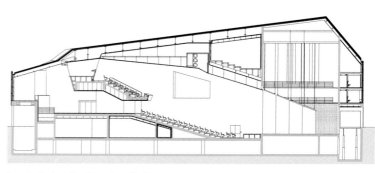

Longitudinal section through auditorium

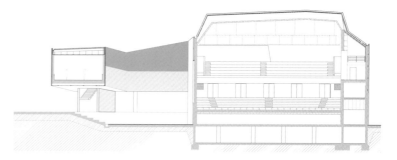

Transverse section through auditorium and administrative level

Construction photos

Rendered view of auditorium

Euskotren Headquarters Development

Durango, Vizcaya

Situated in the industrial town of Durango, in a valley amid three rivers, Zaha Hadid and Patrik Schumacher's new Euskotren Headquarters Development was conceived as a catalyst for the transformation of the town center, once divided by street-level train tracks. The new headquarters, which rises from a low-level structure at its tail to a cantilevering tower at its head, relocates the tracks underground and integrates the subterranean train station with commercial space and an office tower above.

The architects derived the unique contour of the structure and surrounding green spaces by studying paths of vehicular and pedestrian traffic. While the topography appears to be continuous—the tail of the building seems to be an extension of both the tower and the landscape—the elements remain spatially distinct. Morphological manipulations sculpt the ground plane to create outdoor play areas, recreational fields, and an amphitheater. In combination with a series of footpaths, these manipulations guide movement and create a series of separations and connections across the site.

The building proceeds from public to private use as it rises in height: the midheight levels comprise commercial space while the tower is dedicated to private offices. The subterranean train station, situated at the center of the complex and illuminated by a skylight from above, functions as the organizing component of the site. The long north–south orientation of the headquarters maximizes the daylight in the tower and commercial spaces. Both will be clad with an interior curtain wall and an outer open metal mesh for shading and climate control. The skylight above the train station creates a visual and tectonic transition between the metal mesh tower above and the concrete base below.

—TDC

ABOVE: Site plan detail
OPPOSITE: Rendered view from west

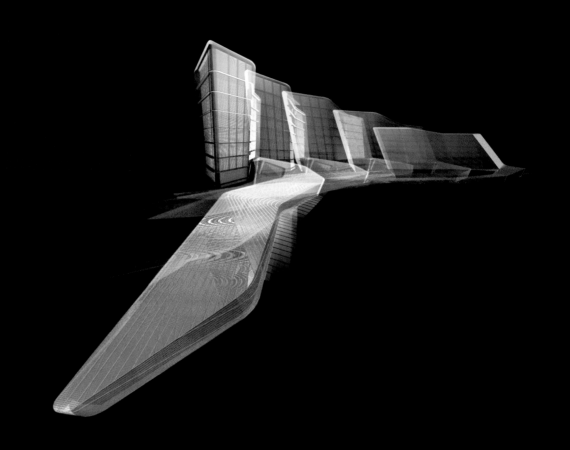

Site plan and section

Plan, ground level and section through terminal

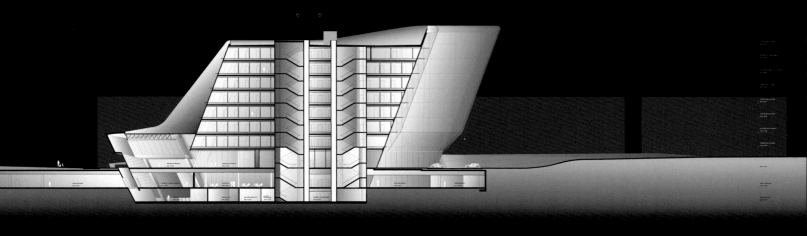

SECCIÓN GG

Section through north offices

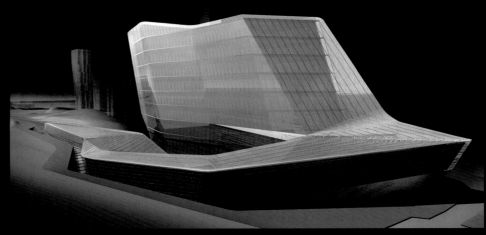

Rendered view from east

Rendered view of commercial entry

Aerial rendering looking into terminal

ABOVE: Rendered view of platform
LEFT: Rendered interior view toward roof of train station

University of Vigo New Campus

Vigo

Jesús Irisarri Castro and Guadalupe Piñera Manso's reconfiguration of the University of Vigo campus, consisting of the addition of several buildings and a rethinking of the overall grounds, is a skillful master plan that solidifies the pair's reputation as an important emerging voice in Spain. Located in Pontevedra, a province in the northern region of Galicia, the university sits on a flat, low-lying plot of land that is flanked by the Pontevedra River and a highway. Consequently, the campus remains relatively cut off from its larger semiurban context. The architects exploit this condition in their planning and design, further exaggerating the idea of an isolated haven with facilities for focused research, intimate instruction, and social and athletic enrichment.

Irisarri and Piñera place a trio of buildings on the site's northern end, closest to the highway. In effect, the buildings become a series of inhabitable barriers between the busy city and the tranquil setting of the campus. The riverside is left sheltered and undeveloped and provides land that, as its own mini-ecosystem, functions as auxiliary scientific research space as well as a place for students to gather and socialize.

The buildings take on the form of three low-lying, fingerlike structures housing a different programmatic need: classrooms, dormitories, and athletic facilities. Though the buildings are separate, they crook and connect at important junctures, allowing distinct facets of campus life to constantly engage with one another. The interstitial spaces between them become the unprogrammed space where more improvisational events may occur. Formally, the three buildings lead one's view toward a building—seven stories tall and highly transparent from the outside—that becomes the architectural centerpiece of the campus. Housing research facilities and classrooms on its upper floors and a theater and entertainment spaces on its ground and subterranean levels, the structure is a beacon of both academic and recreational activity. The enclosed spaces within the glass cladding animate the reading of the interior space, further accentuating the strategies the architects use to both sequester spaces as well as create visual linkages with others.

Irisarri and Piñera's design for the University of Vigo is an honest and straightforward approach to campus planning. In maneuvering both barriers and linkages on the site, the architects develop the notion of a cloistered campus community to its full potential.

—PC

Aerial rendering from east

Rendered view of complex from west

South elevation

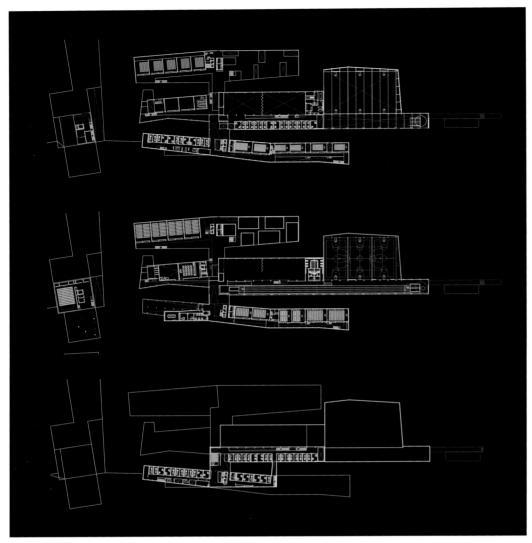

TOP TO BOTTOM: Complex plan, floor 2; complex plan, ground floor; complex plan, sublevel

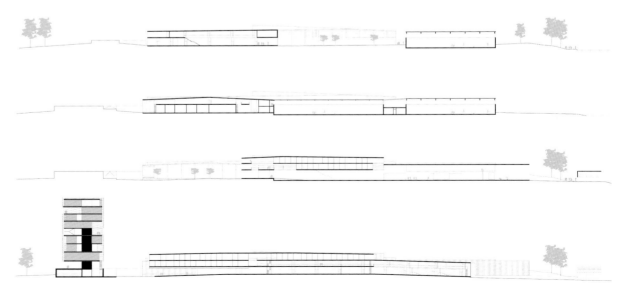

Longitudinal sections

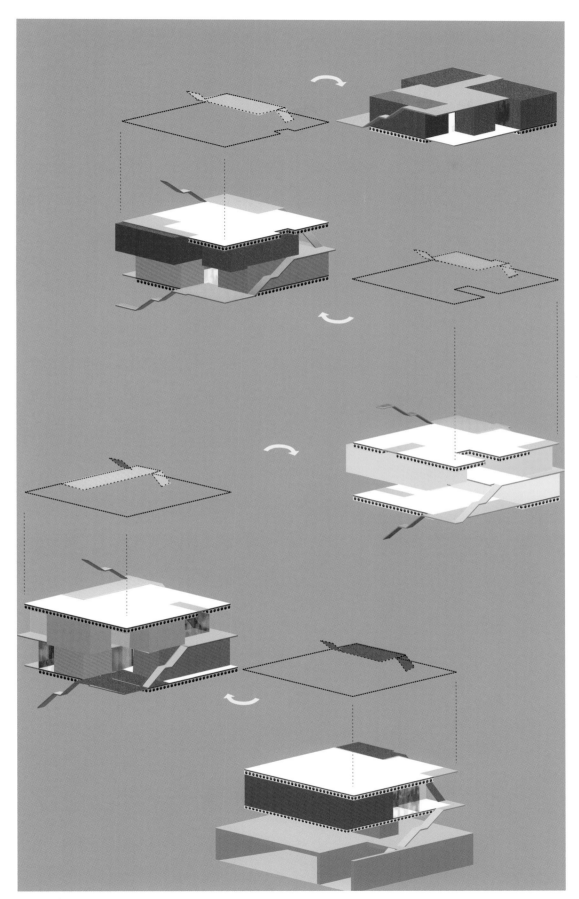

Diagram of interior programs

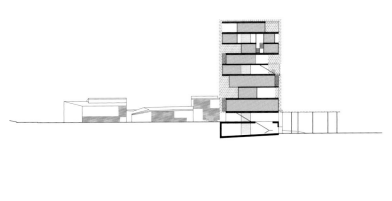

Transverse sections

Rendered view of complex from east

Rendered view along athletics building from west

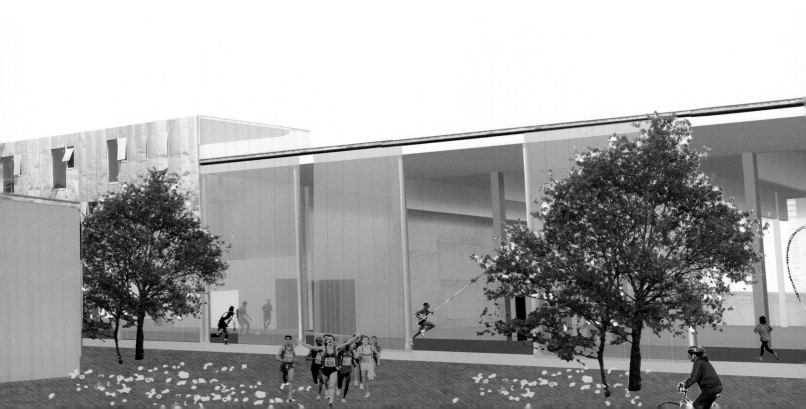

Torre Agbar (2005)

Barcelona

224 | 225

Pamplona

BaluArte Congress Center and Auditorium (2003)

Casa Rural

Girona

Casa Rural, by Catalan architects Rafael Aranda, Carme Pigem, and Ramón Vilalta, is a noteworthy investigation of modern living in a rural setting. Located in an agricultural part of Spain's mountainous northeast corner, close to the French border, the area is characterized by sprawling farmland and few people. Perched on an embankment situated between two pastures, the house, built for a couple and their three children, consists of eleven booths resting on that mound, looking toward the vast, flat farmland. From a distance the volumes, clad in weathered, rust-colored steel, resemble a row of traditional agricultural sheds. Upon closer inspection, they emerge as contemporary inhabitable spaces whose dialectic between primitive shelter and modern dwelling becomes increasingly apparent.

The house is approached from the higher, southern field, where a subterranean tunnel that brings the driver into a garage located in the house's lowest level is carved into the hillock. Both stairs and an elevator lead to the main level. The interior part is quite simple—eleven disparate volumes connected by an interior passageway sunken 5 feet below the crest of the embankment. Each volume functions as a solitary and meditative capsule for private spaces, including bedrooms and bathrooms. Operable partitions lend the hallway and the volumes the flexibility to transition from relatively cellular units into larger related spaces. The southern edge of the house meets the higher field through a series of pitched trays that contain gardens, ponds, and walkways, bringing grass and other vegetation into the house and blurring the spatial relationship between inside and outside. It is on this less partitioned side that communal spaces are embedded, including the living room and kitchen. By being slightly sunken into the earth, this part of the house attains a reclusive, secure character.

"Prospect and refuge," a concept introduced into anthropological and architectural discourse by British geographer Jay Appleton, refers to humans' instinctive need for spaces with expansive views of their surroundings as well as spaces of shelter and protection. Particularly important in the realm of housing, the notion is one that frequently resonates in the best domestic architecture. Casa Rural, with its subterranean dugout and simple, vernacular volumes in tandem with its emancipated, thoroughly modern composition, embodies this notion to its full potential.

—PC

Conceptual sketch

Rendered view of embankment and booths from northeast

Site plan

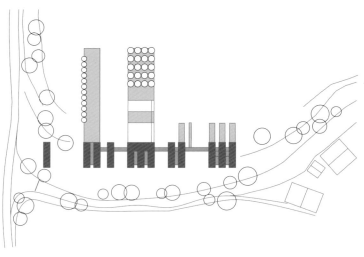

Site plan, detail

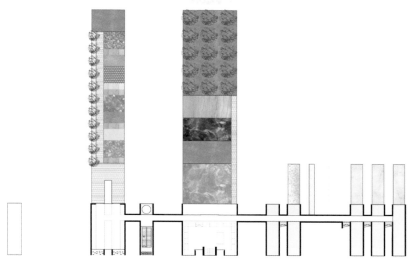

Plan, garden level

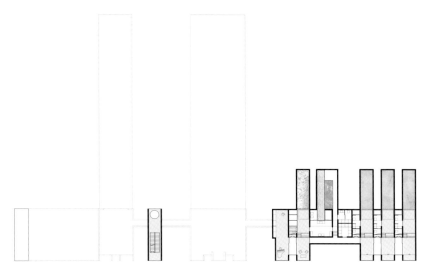

Plan, subterranean level 1

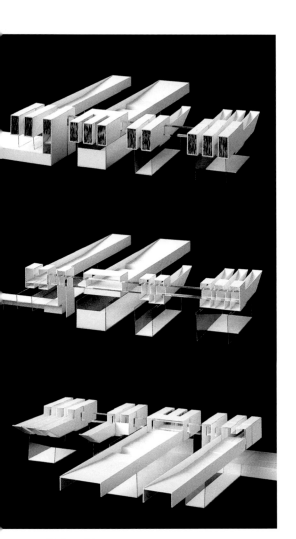

Study models

Plan, subterranean level 2 (garage)

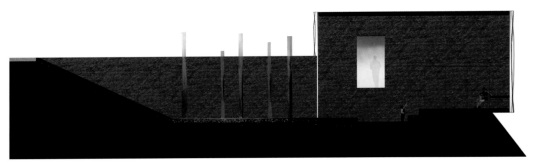

Section through sunken garden

Booth elevation

Rendered view of pasture from north

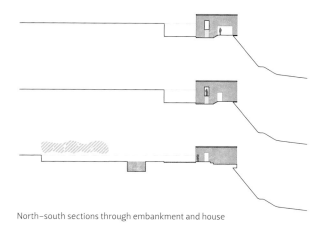

North–south sections through embankment and house

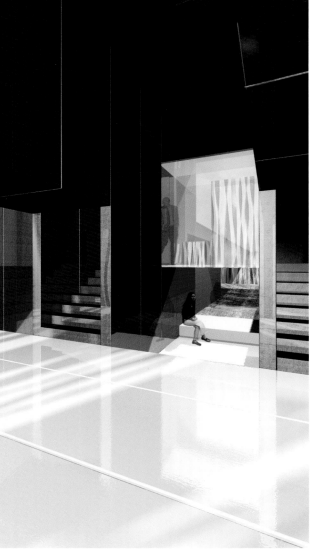

Rendered interior view of booth

Rendered interior view of corridor

Congress and Exhibition Center

Ávila

Francisco Mangado's Congress and Exhibition Center creates a new paradigm for public space in the fortified town of Ávila. To stave off Moorish invaders in the twelfth century, Christians built a wall encircling the town. This rampart, one of the finest remnants of medieval Europe, has continued to delimit and densify the growth of the city. Within the town walls, public spaces are rare and small. Though its medieval structure is Ávila's main draw as a tourist destination, such historical vestiges simultaneously hinder its ability to function as a contemporary city—one in which a sizable public meeting space seems sorely absent.

Lying just outside the walls at the town's northwest corner is a tract of land that was once a riverbed and later a cattle market. The granite-studded soil in this area of Castilla y León is particularly difficult to excavate, so much

of what is built on it must, more or less, rest on the natural contours of the site. Mangado uses this parameter to create a two-part building with two distinct geometries. Resting on the flatter northern part of the site lies the larger component, a simple rectangular volume punctuated by orthogonal protrusions of varying heights. Inside this volume are the center's main hall and auditorium. The main hall has an unconventional orientation in which two raked audiences flank a central stage, while the auditorium has a more traditional proscenium orientation. The two tallest protrusions house rafters in which backdrops are hung before being lowered to the stages. From the exterior, the protrusions echo the geometry of the rampart's gates, dotting its perimeter. The vast, uninterrupted stone facade also conjures a striking resemblance to the city's walls. The smaller component to the south is on more

precipitous topography. This unit appears as an eccentric appendage to its neighbor, functioning as a generous foyer and set of exhibition spaces. The folded, irregular roof abstractly alludes to the site's preexisting, downward pitch.

Mangado's Congress and Exhibition Center is a stunning example of the architect's ability to reinvent charged historical settings, a benchmark of his work. In bringing an important urban space outside the town's walls, the architect tempers crucial historical nods with more abstract inclinations. By giving each impulse a life of its own, Mangado creates a dynamic organism that is simultaneously self-referential and contextual.

—PC

Sketch

Rendered view of exterior showing city wall

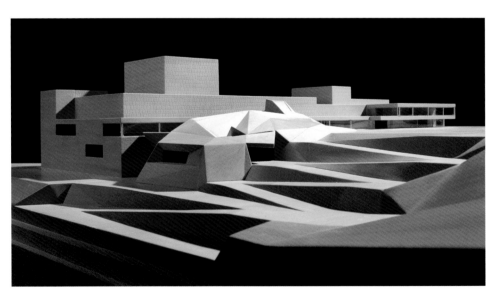

Model, view from southwest toward gallery and main entry

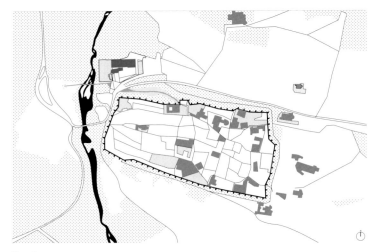

Site plan

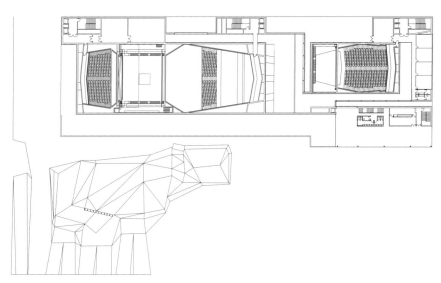

Plan, upper level through both auditoriums

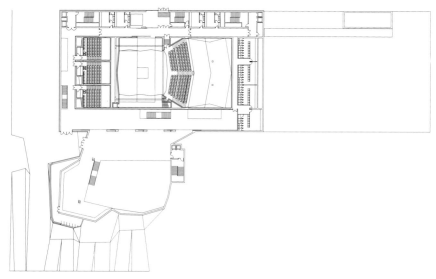

Plan, ground floor showing gallery and main auditorium

Rendered view, exterior entry plaza

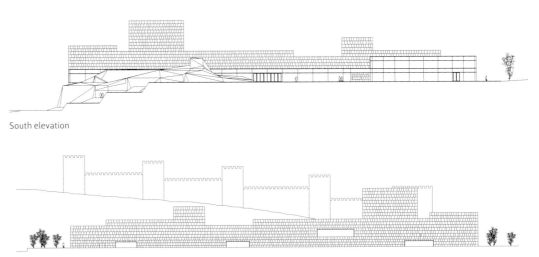

South elevation

North elevation

Rendered view, gallery lobby

Rendered view from interior looking toward city wall

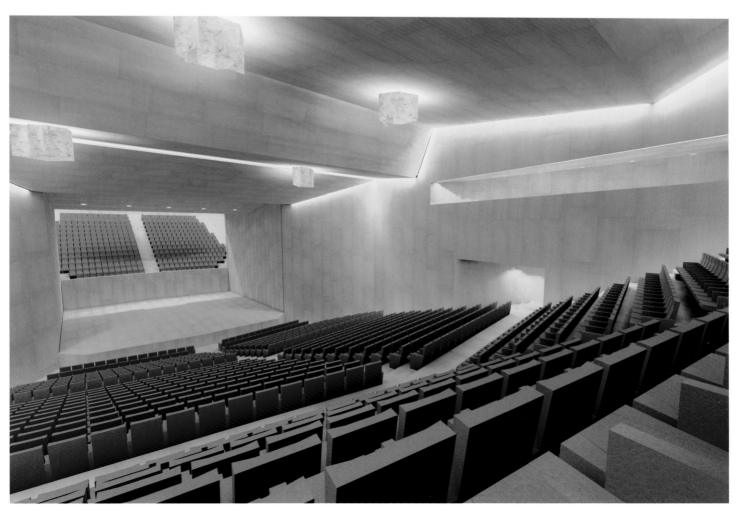

Rendered view of main auditorium

Gas Natural Headquarters

Barcelona

Enric Miralles and Benedetta Tagliabue's design for the new Barcelona headquarters of Spain's Gas Natural company is a formal response to the meeting of multifarious urban forces upon its site. A group of distinct volumes are combined within a single building, creating a fragmented form that breaks down the overall mass of the building, and allowing its different components to address the varied physical context.

The building's primary program is to create office space, which is split between two large volumes: a 282-foot slender high-rise and a horizontal volume nearly equal in length. Nicknamed the "aircraft carrier," the cantilevered horizontal arm is supported by steel trusses hung from a single vertical column. Meeting spaces are contained within the scalloped corbel-like element protruding between the perpendicular office volumes, and the four levels at the base of the building house more offices. A gap between these fragments makes way for a steep internal shaft of light that forms an atrium as well as an entrance lobby and exhibition space.

The facade is subdivided in a manner similar to the building's form. The horizontal transom line is broken and shifted, creating an irregular patchwork grid that disrupts the continuity of the envelope while emphasizing the building's verticality. Slight distortions to the skin's mirrored-glass surface produce abstract, sinuous reflections of the environs.

Located in Barceloneta, a section of Barcelona's waterfront that projects out into the sea, the Gas Natural Headquarters is visible from various points throughout the city down the long boulevards of Ildefons Cerdà's Eixample urban plan and the monumental axis of Barcelona's Arc de Triomf. In the positioning of its forms, the project also addresses the new urban axis of the seafront bypass that runs between the site and the rest of the city. The building's vertical element makes it part of a group of new tower structures that have gone up in recent years, while its smaller volumes tie it to the low-rise residences of the surrounding neighborhood. Planted knolls and fountains in the surrounding plaza form both a terminus for the Barceloneta waterfront promenade and a link to the neighboring park.

—AQ

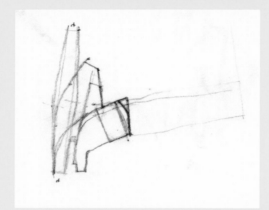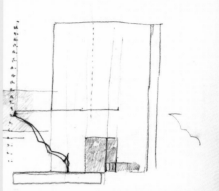

ABOVE: Sketches
OPPOSITE: View from west

Plan, floor 20

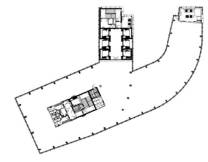

Plan, floor 12

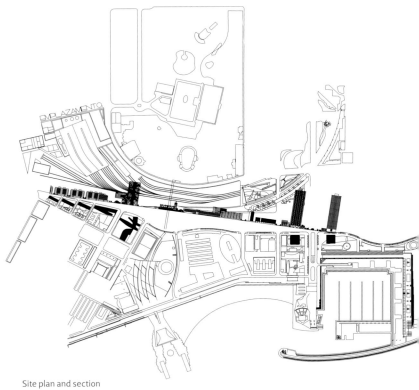

Site plan and section

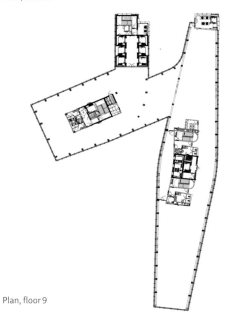

Plan, floor 9

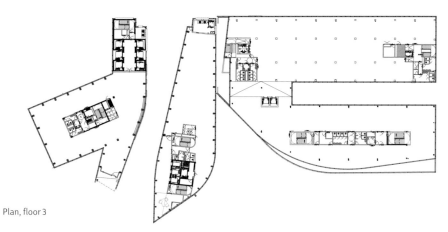

Plan, floor 3

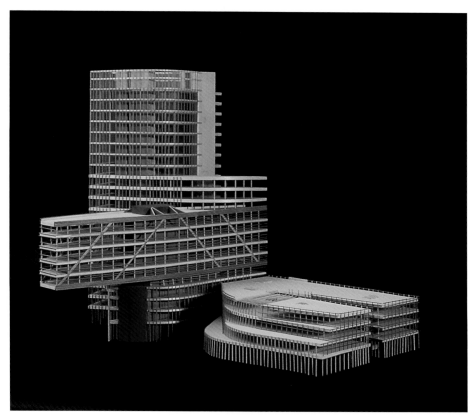

Model

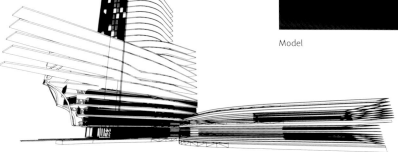

Perspective view

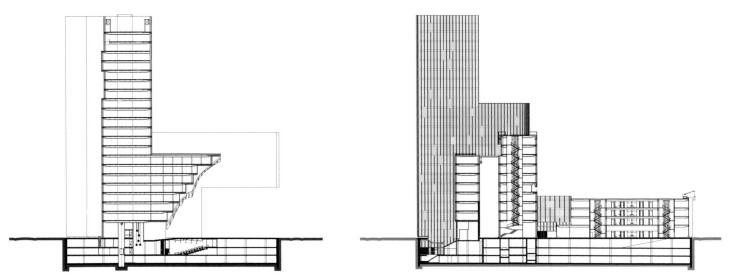

Transverse section through cantilevered volume   North–south section

Model detail

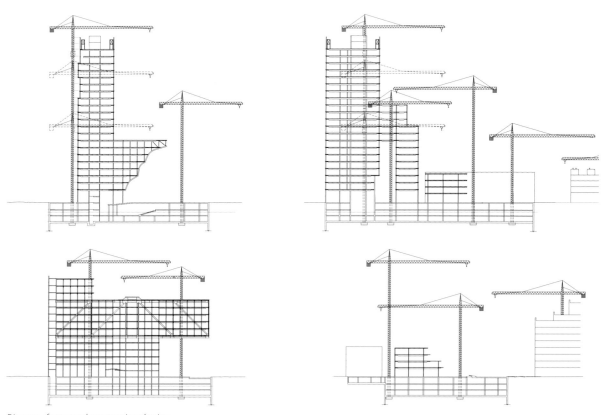

Diagram of structural construction phasing

Photomontage of construction from plaza

Photomontage of construction from beneath bridge

Congress Center

Badajoz

José Selgas and Lucía Cano's Congress Center in Badajoz is an arresting addition to the city's weathered and war-torn landscape. Located in the far reaches of western Extremadura, a stone's throw from the Portuguese border, Badajoz is a time capsule of medieval Spain. Enduring continued attacks from the Portuguese, French, and British until the mid-nineteenth century, Badajoz, perhaps even more than Spain's many other fortified cities, is characterized by militaristic architecture, including huge stone walls, moats, drawbridges, and watchtowers. Modern day Badajoz enjoys a more peaceful, pastoral existence as well as a thriving economy, afforded by its position as a major outpost for Spanish-Portuguese trade.

Bursting out of its historic boundaries, the city is looking for ways to expand without sacrificing its famed landmarks. The Congress Center, embedded into the pentagonal perimeter of one of the city's ramparts as well as the circular footprint of a seventeenth-century

bullring—one of the most important of these landmarks—harnesses both the symbolic weight and historical prominence of the site. Encompassing nearly 3.5 acres, the site is enclosed by a stack of fiberglass rings that forms a permeable exterior curtain. Within these rings sits a stout, cylindrical volume that in turn houses the main auditorium, creating a circular inner hall that functions as the center's vestibule and an informal gathering space. Placed into this entry hall are several stairways that follow the gentle curvature of the auditorium's perimeter as they lead to offices and auxiliary spaces above. The area between the outer ring's eastern edge

and the surrounding rampart is filled in to create smaller subterranean meeting rooms.

The concrete and steel structure will be given a brightly colored acrylic finish, lending the building a playful quality. At night, light emanating from the main auditorium and filtered through the outer fiberglass screen will make the building resemble, at first glance, little more than a folly or sculpture. Selgas and Cano have created a distinctive presence that slips effortlessly into this charged space while cleverly negotiating the trappings of the historic setting.

—PC

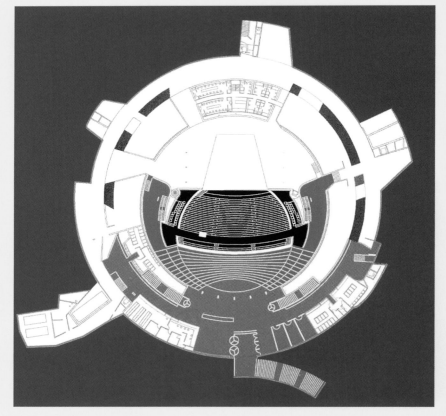

Plan, entry level

Aerial construction photo

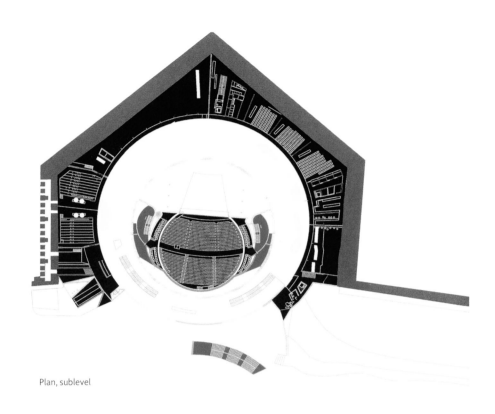

Plan, sublevel

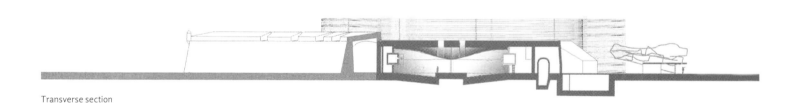

Transverse section

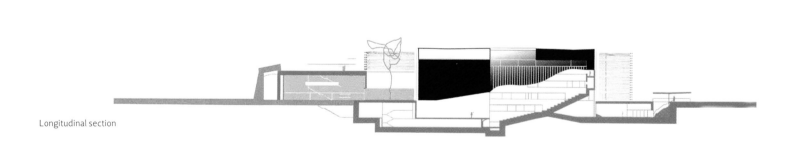

Longitudinal section

Rendered view, stairway

Rendered view, vestibule

Rendered view of stairway

Construction photo, exterior

City Square and Mixed-Use Development

Barakaldo, Vizcaya

The proposed mixed-use development for Barakaldo was a winning entry is Europan 6, a competition for young architects in Europe. The central objective of the project—a collaborative work by Javier Fresneda, Javier Sanjuan, and Javier Peña—is to create a fresh urban identity for Barakaldo, which sits about five miles outside Bilbao on Spain's northern coast.

Barakaldo was historically the center for iron- and steel-making in the region, and the city bears the traces of its industrial past. The development, which includes the refurbishment of the Plaza Pormetxeta and a new tower structure, aims to revitalize Calle Pormetxeta, which extends from the city center to the boulevard running parallel to a nearby estuary where the Nervión River empties into the Bay of Biscay. The new square will anchor these two streets where they meet, forming a vital urban focus.

The square, which accommodates public and retail uses, takes advantage of existing topography in its bi-level plaza space. The lower level of the plaza is an expansive continuous surface that sets the stage for civic interaction, while the ramped upper levels form paths for linear movement across the site.

Pormetxeta Tower stands above the square and comprises three main elements: a plinth, a horizontal arm, and a vertical arm. The plinth forms a base for the other two elements, linking them to the plaza; offices, restaurants, and commercial space are distributed throughout

its three levels. The horizontal arm aligns with the boulevard, mediating between the urban fabric and this new construction. The five levels of this low-rise structure contain housing with staggered vertical circulation cores that act as structural supports, freeing space for a public atrium below. The vertical arm of the tower rises twenty levels above the plinth, bending slightly in a gesture toward the estuary. Each floor of the vertical building accommodates two dwellings with sweeping views over the landscape. The tower is clad in polycarbonate and laminated glass embedded with color, rendering a vibrant translucent skin for this urban beacon.

—AQ

Site plan

Rendered view of plaza from south looking toward tower

Plan, plinth level

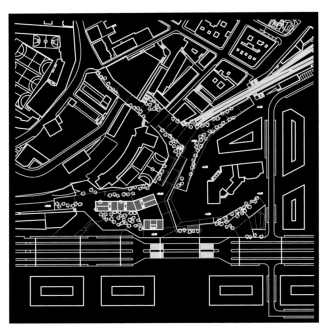

Plan, typical level through both towers

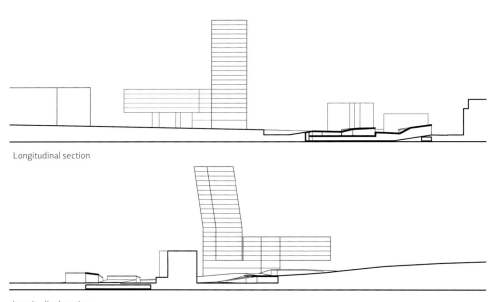

Longitudinal section

Longitudinal section

Transverse section

Competition model, view from above

Competition model, view of plaza from plinth

Rendered view showing plinths, ramps, and gardens

Model, view from east down Calle Pormetxeta

Rendered view from south looking across boulevard, nighttime

Central Library

Jerez de la Frontera, Cádiz

The Central Library in Jerez de la Frontera, Cádiz, designed by José Morales and Sara Giles, faces onto a small public park in this southern city. The architects liken the U-shaped building to a "half-open hand" that cups the park in front, drawing it into the heart of the building while creating a more solid boundary between it and the private buildings behind.

This formal gesture generates a spatial progression that leads visitors from the park through the open court of the building and then inside. The interior spaces are ordered by degree of activity, with the busiest and loudest zones situated closest to the entrance and to the sounds of the park outside. On one side of the entry, a children's activity area looks out toward the green; on the other, the space for browsing newspapers and periodicals leads up to an open-air reading mezzanine on the rear face of the library. This mezzanine forms a solid base that shields interior spaces from noise and elevates the quiet reading areas above the distractions of the outside world. The rear face of the building thus becomes a closed service zone, in contrast to the open filter facing the park in front. A vertical circulation spine at the back of the building connects all floors of the building, from the offices on the top floor above the mezzanine down through the basement, where cultural activities are accommodated in the auditorium and exhibition gallery. Clad in steel panels, the library's exterior walls will have a silvery luster.

The library is organized around pedestrian movement, both inside and out. Ramps lead from the ground floor to book stacks, reading rooms, and a circulation desk on upper levels, guiding visitors in a winding movement up through the building. These switchbacks provide alternating views out through horizontal bands of windows and then back into the heart of the building, reinforcing the relationship between the library and the surrounding park. Rather than compartmentalize programs into enclosed rooms, the architects have created a folded continuous space that is activated and defined by those who use it.

—AQ

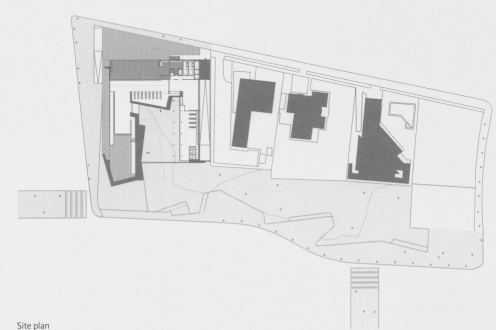

Site plan

Rendered panorama of site from northwest

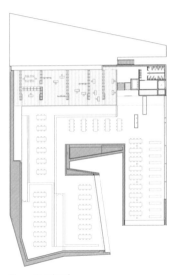

Plan, upper level

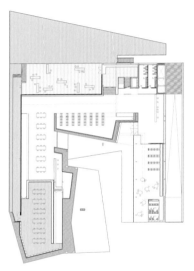

Plan, ground level

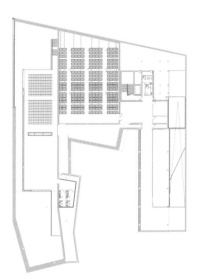

Plan, subterranean level

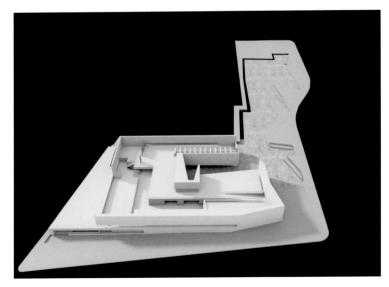

Rendering showing ground level

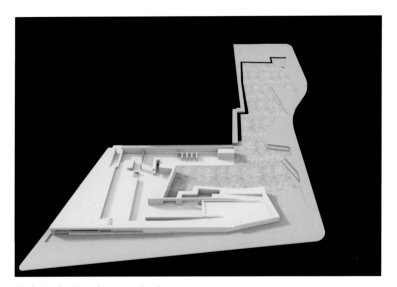

Rendering showing subterranean level

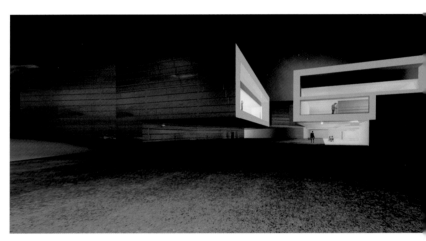

Rendered view of exterior from west, nighttime

Rendered view of exterior from north

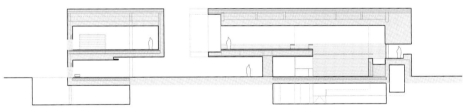

Transverse section

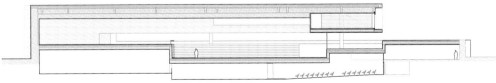

Longitudinal section

Public Housing

Carabanchel, Madrid

Thom Mayne's highly inventive Public Housing, located in Carabanchel, a southern suburban neighborhood of Madrid characterized by towering generic apartment blocks, challenges the prevalent order of Spanish social housing. Mayne proposes a J-shaped typology: a central low-rise village bounded by a slender tower to the north and a mid-rise building to the south. By incorporating elements of traditional detached villas—loggias, green paces, and domestic scale—into a large-scale project, the architect radically transforms the anonymous character of the conventional low-income housing block.

A precast concrete grid forms the lattice-work of the folded facade, which is overlaid with landscape on all sides and interspersed with a series of differently sized openings to relieve the institutional feel of the complex. Large communal gardens punctuate the low-rise village; shared courtyards are placed intermittently throughout the mid-rise building; and smaller private patios are contained inside the individual units. Trees, vegetation-infused pergolas, and trellises cover the central paseo that leads from the north to the south buildings, replacing the traditional interior lobby and transforming this area into a public plaza and open entry. Parking is housed below ground. Individual residences range from three- and four-bedroom units in the village to two-bedroom and one- and two-floor three-bedroom units in the tower.

—TDC

Study model

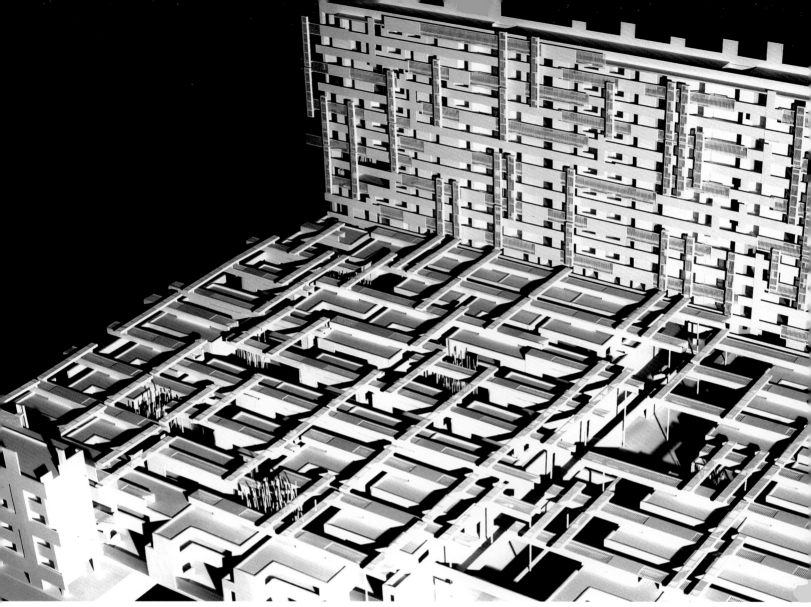

Rendered view from above

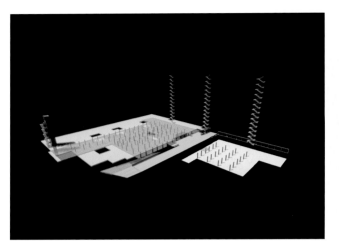

Diagram, main public entry and plaza

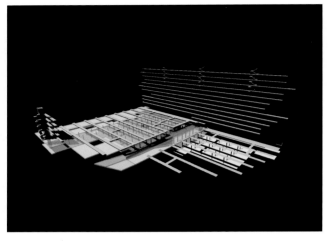

Diagram, circulation

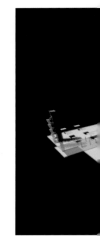

Diagram, patio system

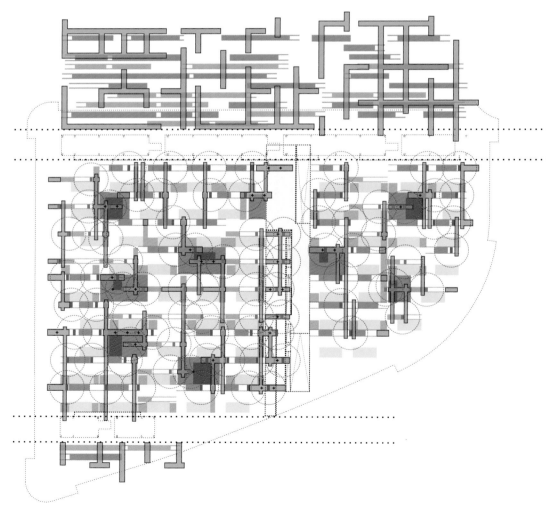

ABOVE AND OPPOSITE: Diagrams of material units

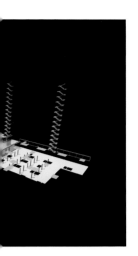
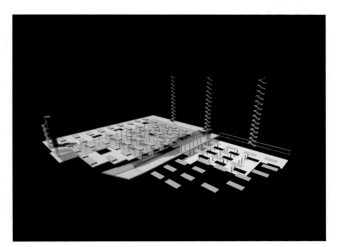

Diagram, terrace system

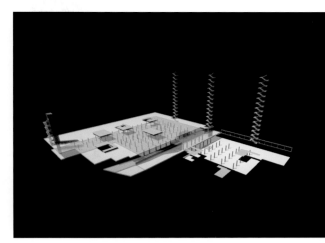

Diagram, public spaces

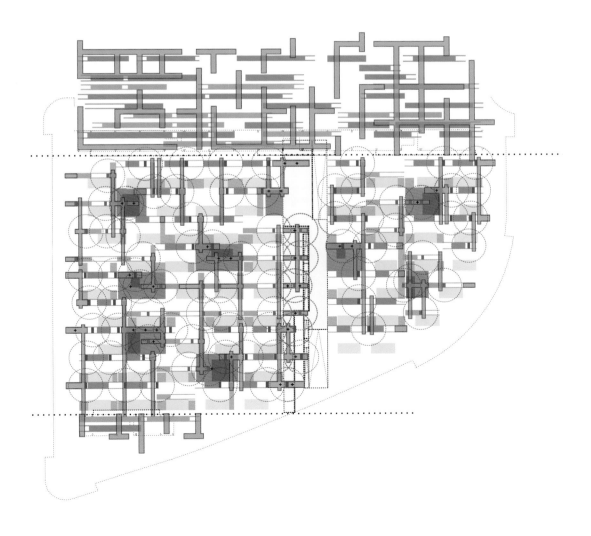

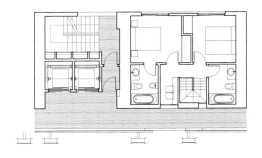

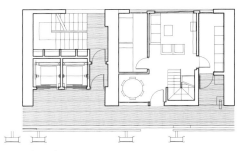

Typical unit plans

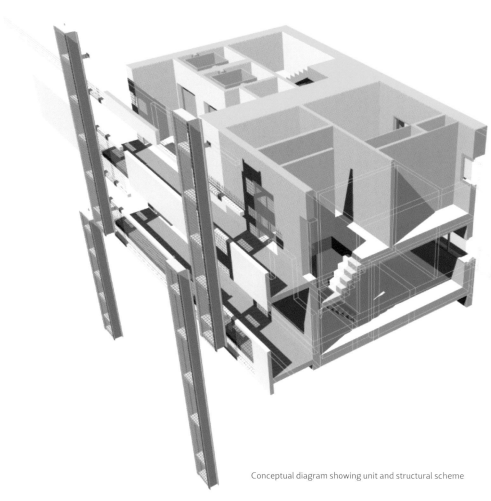

Conceptual diagram showing unit and structural scheme

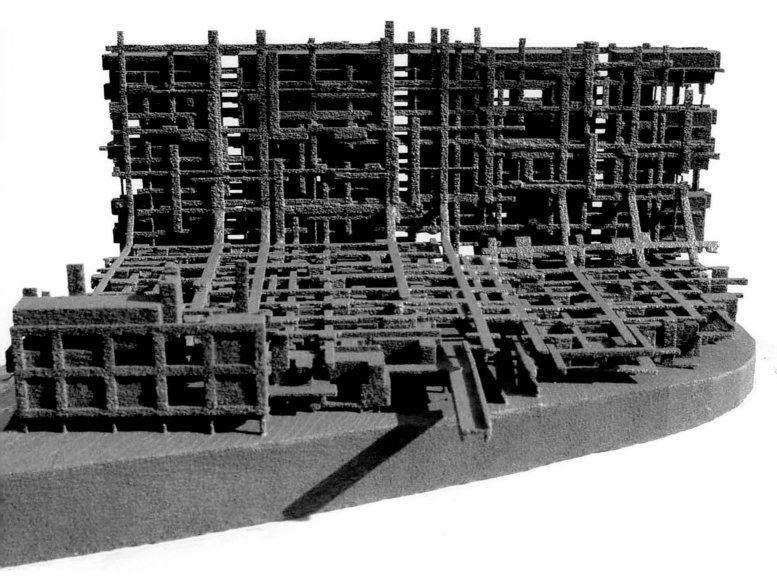

Study model

Study model detail

Tenerife North Airport (2002)

La Laguna, Tenerife

Edificio Mirador (2005)

Sanchinarro, Madrid

José Antonio Martinez Lapeña and Elías Torres Tur   I   Martinez Lapeña–Torres, Arquitectos

Toledo

La Granja Escalators (2000)

Selected Bibliography

COMPILED BY PETER CHRISTENSEN

The following is a select listing of recent and notable publications and articles about the architects whose works are featured in this publication. Citations are listed in reverse chronological order; multiple listings from the same year are listed alphabetically.

Abalos&Herreros
Ábalos, Iñaki, and Juan Herreros. *Grand Tour*. Madrid: Centro Atlantico de Arte Moderno, Las Palmas de Gran Canaria Fundación ICO, 2005.
———. *Tower and Office. From Modernist Theory to Contemporary Practice*. Cambridge, Mass.: The MIT Press, 2005.
"Abalos&Herreros: Recent Work." *2G*, no. 22 (2002).
Ábalos, Iñaki, Juan Herreros, and Ignasi de Sola Morales. *Recycling Madrid*. Barcelona: Actar, 2001.
Ábalos, Iñaki, and Juan Herreros. *Natural Artificial*. Madrid: EXIT Editores. Liga Multimedia Internacional, 1999.

Acebo X Alonso Arquitectos
"Work Systems." *El Croquis*, no. 119 (2004): 36–75.
"M-U House, House in La Moraleja, Camara House, Palma de Mallorca Fair Complex, A Coruña Arts Centre." *El Croquis*, nos. 106–07 (2001): 300–21.

Álvaro Siza 2 Arquitecto
Molteni, Francesco, and Alessandra Cianchetta. *Álvaro Siza: Private Houses*. Milan: Skira, 2005.
Jodidio, Philip. *Álvaro Siza*. Revised edition. Cologne: Taschen, 2003.
"Álvaro Siza 1958–2000." *El Croquis*, no. 95 (2000).
Frampton, Kenneth. *Álvaro Siza*. London and New York: Phaidon, 2000.
Angelillo, Antonio. *Alvaro Siza: Writings on Architecture*. Milan: Skira, 1998.

AMP Arquitectos
"Megalito Urbano." *Arquitectura Viva*, no. 101 (2005): 74–83.
Artengo-Menis-Pastrana et al. *AMP Arquitectos Artengo-Menis-Pastrana*. Barcelona: Actar, 2000.

Aranguren&Gallegos
ACCIONES: *Aranguren & Gallegos Works, 1995–2004*. Madrid: Editorial Rueda, 2004.
ARANGUREN + GALLEGOS: WORKS. Pamplona: T6 Ediciones, 2000.

Ateliers Jean Nouvel
"Jean Nouvel." *El Croquis*, nos. 112–13 (2003).
"Jean Nouvel." *L'Architecture d'aujourd'hui*, no. 237 (2001).
Bosoni, Giampiero. *Jean Nouvel: Architecture and Design 1976–1995*. Milan: Skira, 1998.
Morgan, Conway Lloyd. *Jean Nouvel: The Elements of Architecture*. New York: Universe, 1998.
Boissière, Olivier. *Jean Nouvel*. Paris: Vilo International, 1997.

b720 Arquitectos
Bonet, Llorenc. *New Houses: Thirty-six of the World's Most Spectacular Home Designs*. New York: Harper Collins, 2005.

Carlos Ferrater Partnership
"Carlos Ferrater: Recent Work." *2G*, no. 32 (2004).
Preziosi, Massimo. *Carlos Ferrater: Works and Projects*. London: Phaidon, 2002.
Curtis, William J. R., Harm Tilman, and Ricard Fayos. *Carlos Ferrater*. Barcelona: Actar, 2001.
Ferrater, Carlos. *Thicker Than Paper: Congress Center of Catalonia*. Barcelona: Actar, 2001.
Da Costa, Alec. *Carlos Ferrater: Building a Public Building*. Modena, Italy: Logos, 1999.

Cloud 9
Ferré, Albert, ed. *Verb Conditioning: The Design of New Atmospheres, Effects, and Experiences*. Barcelona: Actar, 2005.
Guallart, Vicente, et al. *Media House Project: The House Is the Computer, the Structure Is the Network*. Barcelona: Actar, 2003.

Corea Morán Arquitectura
Petterson, Eduard. *Arquitectura Minimalista*. Barcelona: Atrium Group, 2004.
Maki, Fumihiko. *Corea-Gallardo-Mannino*. Madrid: Aspan, 1993.

David Chipperfield Architects
"David Chipperfield Architectural Works 1998–2004." *El Croquis*, no. 120 (2004).
Chipperfield, David. *David Chipperfield*. Princeton, N.J.: Princeton Architectural Press, 2003.
———. *Theoretical Practice*. London: Artemis, 1994.

Dominique Perrault Architecture
Capitanucci, Maria Vittoria. *Dominique Perrault: Recent Works*. Milan: Skira, forthcoming.
de Bure, Gilles. *Dominique Perrault*. In French and English. Paris: Vilo International, 2004.
"Dominique Perrault." *a+u*, no. 391 (2003).
Perrault, Dominique. *Dominique Perrault*. Basel: Birkhäuser, 1999.

Eisenman Architects
Eisenman Architects. *Code X: City of Culture of Galicia*. Edited by Cynthia Davidson. New York: Monacelli Press, 2005.
———. *Holocaust Memorial Berlin*. Baden, Germany: Lars Müller Publishers, 2005.
Eisenman, Peter. *Barfuss Auf Weiss Gluhenden Mauren/ Barefoot on White-Hot Wall*. Ostfildern, Germany: Hatje Cantz Publishers, 2005.
———. *Eisenman: Inside Out, Selected Writings 1963–1988*. Edited by Mark Rakatansky. New Haven, Conn.: Yale University Press, 2004.
Eisenman Architects. *Blurred Zones: Investigation of the Interstitial. Eisenman Architects 1988–1998*. New York: Monacelli Press, 2003.
Eisenman, Peter. *Diagram Diaries*. New York: Universe, 1999.

EMBT Miralles Tagliabue Arquitectes Associats
Cuito, Aurora. *Miralles Tagliabue: EMBT Architects*. Multilingual edition. New York: Te Neues, 2005.
Miralles, Enric, and Benedetta Tagliabue. *EMBT Enric Miralles Benedetta Tagliabue Work in Progress*. Barcelona: Collegi d'Arquitectes de Catalunya, 2005.
"Enric Miralles Benedetta Tagliabue 1996–2000." *El Croquis*, nos. 100–01 (2000).
Miralles, Enric, and Benedetta Tagliabue. *Enric Miralles Benedetta Tagliabue, Time Architecture*. Barcelona: Gustavo Gili, 1999.
Documenti di Architettura, Enric Miralles, Opere e Progetti. Edited by Benedetta Tagliabue. Milan: Electa, 1996.
Miralles, Enric. *Enric Miralles: Works and Projects 1975–1995*. Edited by Benedetta Tagliabue. New York: Monacelli Press, 1996.

Estudio Arquitectura Campo Baeza
Blanco, Manuel. *Light Is More*. Madrid: T. F. Editores, 2003.
Campo Baeza, Alberto. *Caja General de Ahorros. Granada*. Madrid: Iberica Estar Books, 2003.
———. *La Idea Construida*. Madrid: Colegio Oficial de Arquitectos de Madrid, 1999.
Frampton, Kenneth, Alberto Campo Baeza, and Oscar Riera Ojeda. *Campo Baeza*. Gloucester, Mass.: Rockport Publishers, 1997.

Foreign Office Architects (FOA)
"Complexity and Consistency." *El Croquis*, nos. 115–16 (2003).
Foreign Office Architects (FOA). *Phylogenesis – foa's ark*. Barcelona: Actar, 2003.
———. *The Yokohama Project*. Barcelona: Actar, 2002.
"FOA: Recent Projects." *2G*, no. 16 (2001).

Gehry Partners
Gehry Draws. Edited by Mark Rappolt and Robert Violette. Cambridge, Mass.: The MIT Press, 2004.
Forster, Kurt W., and Francesco Dal Co. *Frank O. Gehry: The Complete Works*. London: Phaidon, 2003.
Gehry, Frank. *Symphony: Frank Gehry's Walt Disney Concert Hall*. New York: Harry N. Abrams, 2003.
Friedman, Mildred. *Gehry Talks: Architecture and Process*. New York: Universe, 2002.
Lindsey, Bruce. *Digital Gehry*. Cologne: Birkhäuser, 2002.
Gehry, Frank O. *Design and Architecture*. Weil am Rhein, Germany: Vitra Design Museum, 1996.

GPY arquitectos
González Pérez, Juan Antonio, Constanze Sixt, and Urbano Yanes Tuña. *GPY Arquitectos 2005*. Santa Cruz de Tenerife: Gobierno de Canarias and Consejería de Educación, Cultura y Deportes, 2005.
Hernández de León, Miguel. *Conjugar Los Vacíos. Ensayos de Arquitectura*. Madrid: Abada Editores, 2005.

Guallart Architects
Guallart, Vicente. *Media, Mountains, and Architecture*. Barcelona: Actar, forthcoming.
———. *geoCat: Territorial Loops/Territoris Enllacats*. Barcelona: Actar, 2005.
Guallart, Vicente, et al. *The Media House Project*. Barcelona: Actar, 2005.
Guallart, Vicente. *Sociopolis*. Barcelona: Actar, 2004.
"Intelligent Realities." *Design Document Series*, no. 3 (2004).

Guillermo Vázquez Consuegra
Vázquez Consuegra. Saggio di V. Pérez Escolano. Documenti di Architettura. Milan: Electa, 2005.
Vázquez Consuegra. Introduction by Peter Buchanan. Barcelona: Gustavo Gili, 1992.

Herzog & de Meuron
Herzog & de Meuron: Natural History. Edited by Philip Ursprung. Baden, Germany: Lars Müller Publishers, 2005.
Mack, Gerhard. *Herzog & de Meuron 1992–1996: The Complete Works*. Vol. 3. Cologne: Birkhäuser, 2001.
Herzog & de Meuron: 15 Built Projects 1988–1999. Cologne: Birkhäuser, 2000.
"Herzog & de Meuron 1981–2000." *El Croquis*, nos. 60/84 (2000).
Mack, Gerhard. *Herzog & de Meuron 1978–1988: The Complete Works*. Vol. 1. Cologne: Birkhäuser, 1997.
———. *Herzog & de Meuron 1989–1991: The Complete Works*. Vol. 2. Cologne: Birkhäuser, 1996.

irisarri + piñera
Bradbury, Dominic. *New Country Houses*. London: Laurence King, 2004.
Cohn, David. *Young Spanish Architects*. Basel: Birkhäuser, 2000.

J.MAYER H.
Mayer H., Jürgen. *Metropol Parasol*. Berlin: Andres Lepik and Staatliche Museen zu Berlin, 2005.
Rosa, Joseph. *Next Generation: Folds, Blobs, and Boxes*. New York: Rizzoli, 2003.
Mayer H., Jürgen. *Surphase Architecture*. Berlin: Aedes, 2002.

José Maria Torres Nadal
Metápolis, Diccionario de Arquitectura Avanzada. Barcelona: Actar, 2002.
Torres Nadal, José Maria. *Arquitecturas de Autor: José Maria Torres Nadal*. Pamplona: T6 Ediciones, 1998.

Josep Lluís Mateo – MAP Arquitectos
Mateo, Josep Lluís, and Aaron Betsky. *Barcelona International Convention Centre CCIB*. Barcelona: Actar, 2005.
Mateo, Josep Lluís, Jose Luis Pardo, and Philip Ursprung. *Projects, Works, Writings*. Barcelona: Ediciones Polígrafa, 2005.
"Josep Lluís Mateo: Recent Work." *2G*, no. 25 (2002).
Mateo, Josep Lluís, Aaron Betsky, and Claes Caldenby. *Mateo Atlas*. Barcelona: Actar, 1998.

Juan Domingo Santos
"Complexity and Consistency." *El Croquis*, no. 119 (2004): 76–115.
"Recreation and Cultural Centre, Houses Amongst Rubble, Fruit Orchards and Houses." *El Croquis*, nos. 106–07 (2001): 350–69.

Juan Navarro Baldeweg
Navarro Baldeweg, Juan, and Juan Manuel Bonet. *Juan Navarro Baldeweg*. Corte Madera, Calif.: Gingko Press, 2001.
Navarro Baldeweg, Juan. *Juan Navarro Baldeweg*. Madrid: Tanais Ediciones, 2000.
"Juan Navarro Baldeweg." *El Croquis*, no. 73-II (1995).
Lahuerta, Juan José, and Angel González García. *Juan Navarro Baldeweg. Opere e Progetti*. Milan: Electa, 1990.

Kazuyo Sejima + Ryue Nishizawa/SANAA
"SANAA Sejima+Nishizawa." *El Croquis*, nos. 121–22 (2004).
Sejima, Kazuyo, and Ryue Nishizawa. *Kazuyo Sejima + Ryue Nishizawa/SANAA: Works 1995–2003*. Tokyo: Toto, 2003.
Wilkins, Gretchen, Doug Klebaugh, and SANAA. *SANAA: Recent Work. The John Dinkeloo Memorial Lecture*. Ann Arbor: University of Michigan Press, 2003.
Sejima, Kazuyo, and Ryue Nishizawa. *Kazuyo Sejima in Gifu*. Barcelona: Actar, 2002.

Francisco Leiva Ivorra & grupo aranea
Leiva Ivorra, Francisco. *Dibujos, Drawings 1993–2005*. Valencia: ICARO, Colegio Territorial de Arquitectos de Valencia, forthcoming.
———. *Zombi Tour 00*. Alicante, Spain: Editorial Cuarto Menguante, 2005.

Mangado y Asociados
Francisco Mangado, Arquitecto. Valencia: Editorial Biblioteca TC, forthcoming.
Mangado, Francisco. *Francisco Mangado. Obras y Proyectos. Edición Española de Opere e Progetti*. Barcelona: Gustavo Gili, 2005.
Francisco Mangado: Baluarte, Palacio de Congresos y Auditorio de Navarra. Casal de Cambra, Portugal: L. Caleidoscopio, 2004.
Francisco Mangado. Barcelona: Gustavo Gili, 1994.

Mansilla+Tuñón, Arquitectos
Mansilla, Luis M., Emilio Tuñón, and Luis Rojo. *Escritos Circenses*. Barcelona: Gustavo Gili, 2005.
Mansilla, Luis M., and Emilio Tuñón. *MUSAC: The Building*. Barcelona: Actar, 2004.
"Mansilla+Tuñón, Arquitectos." *El Croquis*, nos. 115–16 (2003).
Mansilla+Tuñón. Milan: Electa, 1998.

manuel bailo + rosa rull
Asensio, Paco, and Hugo Kliczkowski. *Nuevas Tiendas y Boutiques*. Santander, Spain: H Kliczkowski, 2005.
V Biennal de Arquitectura Española. Barcelona: Actar and Gustavo Gili, 2005.

Martínez Lapeña – Torres, Arquitectos
Pellegrinni, Pietro Carlo. *Piazza e Spazi Pubblici. Architttetura 1990–2005*. Milan: Federico Motta Editore, 2005.
Guía del Patrimonio Arquitectónico de Eivissa y Formentera. Ibiza: Diario de Ibiza, 2003.

MGM Morales+Giles+Mariscal
Morales, José, Juan González, and Sara de Giles. *MGM Morales Giles Mariscal. En Favor de una Arquitectura Instalada* Madrid: Editorial Rueda, 2004.
———. *Arquitecturas de Autor: Morales, de Giles, G. Mariscal*. Pamplona: T6 Ediciones, 2003.

Morphosis
Mayne, Thom. *Morphosis, 1998–2004*. New York: Rizzoli, forthcoming.
Mayne, Thom, and Val Warke. *Morphosis*. London: Phaidon, 2003.
Kipnis, Jeffrey, and Todd Gannon. *Morphosis: Diamond Ranch High School*. New York: Monacelli Press, 2001.
Vidler, Anthony. *Morphosis: Buildings and Projects 1993–1997*. New York: Rizzoli, 1999.

MTM arquitectos
Monoespacios 2. MTM. Javier Fresneda & Javier Sanjuán. Madrid: Edita Fundación COAM, 2005.

MVRDV
MVRDV. *KM3 – Excursions on Capacity*. Barcelona: Actar, 2005.
"MVRDV Redefining the Tools of Radicalism." *El Croquis*, no. 86 (2004).
Betsky, Aaron, and Winy Maas. *Reading MVRDV*. Rotterdam: NAI Publishers, 2003.
MVRDV. *Costa Iberica: Upbeat to the Leisure City*. Barcelona: Actar, 2000.

Nieto Sobejano Arquitectos
Nieto, Fuensanta, and Enrique Sobejano. *Innovación en Vivienda Social*. Barcelona: Carles Broto I Comerma, 2005.
———. *Arquitecturas de Autor: Nieto Sobejano*. Pamplona: T6 Ediciones, 2004.
———. *NIETO SOBEJANO 1996–2001*. Madrid: Editorial Rueda, 2002.

NO.MAD Arquitectos
"Football Stadium, Barakaldo." *Arquitectura Viva Monographs*, nos. 105–06 (2004).
"Principles of Uncertainty." *El Croquis*, no. 118 (2003): 25–114.
"Villa Olimpica de Paris." *L'Architecture d'aujourd'hui*, no. 339 (2002): 36–37.

N.Tres
Bernardó, Jordi. *Transportes Interurbanos de Tenerife Central Workshop and Offices*. Barcelona: Actar, 2003.

Office for Metropolitan Architecture (OMA)
Koolhaas, Rem. *Content*. Cologne: Taschen, 2004.
———. *Harvard Design School Project on The City 1: Guide to Shopping*. Cologne: Taschen, 2001.
———. *Harvard Design School Project on The City 2: Great Leap Forward*. Cologne: Taschen, 2001.
———. *Projects for Prada Part 1*. Milan: Fondazione Prada Edizioni, 2001.
Koolhaas, Rem, and Bruce Mau. *S, M, L, XL*. New York: Monacelli Press, 1995.
Koolhaas, Rem. *Delirious New York: A Retroactive Manifesto for Manhattan*. New York: Oxford University Press, 1978.

Rafael Moneo
Moneo, Rafael. *Sobre El Concepto de Arbitrariedad en Arquitectura*. Madrid: Real Academia de Bellas Artes de San Fernando, 2005.
———. *Theoretical and Design Strategies in the Work of Eight Contemporary Architects*. Cambridge, Mass.: The MIT Press, 2005.
Rafael Moneo. Museos, Auditorios, Bibliotecas. San Sebastián: Kutxa, 2005.
"Rafael Moneo: Imperative Anthology, 1967–2004." *El Croquis*, nos. 20/64/98 (2004).
Capella, Juli. *Rafael Moneo Diseñador*. Barcelona: Santa & Cole, ETSA, 2003.

RCR Arquitectes
RCR Arquitectes. *Virutal Versus Físoc. Projecte de Creació Multidisciplinària*. Barcelona: Escola Tècnica Superior d'Arquitectura de Barcelona, 2005.
———. *RCR Aranda Pigem Vilalta Arquitectes. Between Abstraction and Nature*. Barcelona: Gustavo Gili, 2004.
———. *Works 1988–98. Aranda Pigem Vilalta Architects*. Tokyo: Critoria, 1998.

Richard Rogers Partnership
Powell, Kenneth. *Richard Rogers: Complete Works*. Vol. 3. London: Phaidon, forthcoming.
———. *Richard Rogers: Complete Works*. Vol. 2. London: Phaidon, 2001.
———. *Richard Rogers: Complete Works*. Vol. 1. London: Phaidon, 1999.
Russell, James, et al. *Pioneering British High-Tech*. Phaidon, 1999.
Rogers, Richard. *Cities for a Small Planet*. Edited by Philip Gumuchdjian. London: Faber and Faber, 1997.

SANCHO-MADRIDEJOS ARCHITECTURE OFFICE
Madridejos, Sol, and J. C. Sancho Osinaga. *Suite en Tres Movimentos. SANCHO-MADRIDEJOS*. Madrid: Ediciones Rueda, 2001.
———. *Arquitecturas de Autor: SANCHO-MADRIDEJOS*. Pamplona: T6 Ediciones, 1996.
Cargill Thompson, Jessica. *40 Architects under 40*. Cologne: Taschen, 2000.

selgascano
"Sistemas de Trabajo." *El Croquis*, no. 119 (2004): 126–50.

Toyo Ito & Associates, Architects
"Toyo Ito, 2001–2005: Beyond Modernism." *El Croquis*, no. 123 (2005).
"Toyo Ito Beyond the Image." *a+u*, no. 417 (June 2005).
Maffei, Andrea. *Toyo Ito: Works, Projects, Writing*. Milan: Electa, 2002.
"Toyo Ito 1970–2001." *GA Architect*, no. 17 (2001).
Ito, Toyo. *Blurring Architecture*. Milan: Charta, 2000.

XPIRAL
"España 6 Barakaldo, Square and Offices in Pormetxeta." In *Europan 7*, p. 192. Madrid: Europan España Secretariat, 2003.

Zaha Hadid Architects
Fontana Giusti, Gordana, and Patrik Schumacher. *Zaha Hadid: The Complete Works*. London: Thames & Hudson, 2004.
Hadid, Zaha, and Peter Giovanni. *Zaha Hadid: Car Park and Terminus Strasbourg*. Baden, Germany: Lars Müller Publishers, 2004.
Schumacher, Patrik. *Digital Hadid*. Basel: Birkhäuser, 2004.
"Zaha Hadid: 1983–2004." *El Croquis*, no. 103 (2004).
Binet, Helene, et al. *Architecture of Zaha Hadid in Photographs by Helene Binet*. Baden, Germany: Lars Müller Publishers, 2000.

Acknowledgments

In the strict sense of the word, I suppose the time I have spent over the years looking at architecture and meeting with architects in Spain might be considered a form of labor. I am grateful to all those architects working in Spain who have ensured—by their talents and their graciousness—that this effort was not only a light burden but also an immensely enjoyable one.

Noted critic and publisher Luis Fernández-Galiano provided ready advice as the project took shape. He also read a draft of my essay and responded with extremely helpful comments and criticism, in addition to writing a concise and insightful preface to this volume.

Glenn D. Lowry, Director of The Museum of Modern Art and a stalwart supporter of this effort from the start, contributed a thoughtful foreword. The book's thirty-five project texts were written by Peter Christensen, Curatorial Assistant, Tina diCarlo, Assistant Curator, and Alexandra Quantrill, Project Curatorial Assistant, Department of Architecture and Design.

This book is one of the first to be printed during the tenure of MoMA's new publisher, Christopher Hudson, and the amazing efforts of his staff in the Department of Publications ensure an auspicious beginning. All of the texts contained herein have benefited from the indefatigable scrutiny of Libby Hruska, who served as the book's conscientious editor. Marc Sapir, Production Director, brought the same tenacity and keen eye to the book's physical qualities as well as its timely completion and delivery.

The design of this book represents the most recent efforts of the Museum's Department of Graphic Design, and its director, Ed Pusz. Hsien-Yin Ingrid Chou, Assistant Director, was the lead designer and deserves credit for the book's handsome and clear design. She is also responsible for ensuring, with the assistance of freelance designer Tamara Maletic, that the design of the book is evident in the exhibition that it accompanies. Thanks also go to Claire Corey, Production Manager, Department of Graphic Design, and Cassandra Heliczer, Associate Editor, Department of Publications, who saw that the production and editing of the exhibition graphics were of the same high quality as those of this book.

Both the book and the exhibition have benefited from the great talent behind the superb images provided by photographer Roland Halbe of Stuttgart, Germany. A frequent visitor to Spain, Halbe not only contributed images from his exceptional inventory but also undertook specially commissioned work for this project, assisted by his invaluable studio manager, Amrei Heyne.

Jerry Neuner, Director of Exhibition Design and Production, and Betty Fisher, Exhibition Designer, ensured that all the data collected and all the ideas projected were brought together and realized in three dimensions to the highest standards. They worked closely with Benjamin Aranda and Chris Lasch of Aranda/Lasch to create the bases for the models, whose complex geometries and high-tech production represent new benchmarks for the Museum's exhibition production.

I would also like to thank Randolph Black, Associate Coordinator, Department of Exhibitions, and Jennifer Russell, Senior Deputy Director for Exhibitions and Collections, for their efforts in keeping this exhibition on track. Sacha Eaton, Senior Registrar Assistant, ensured that the models arrived in one piece and on time. Todd Bishop, Director, Mary Hannah, Assistant Director, Exhibition Funding, and Nicole Goldberg, Assistant Director, Development and Membership, deserve to be recognized for the efforts of the Department of Development.

Meg Blackburn, Senior Publicist, and Kim Mitchell, Director of Communications, have done a great job of bringing the project to the attention of the media locally and internationally. In devising educational programs to accompany the book and exhibition, Gwen Farrelly, Landau Fellow, Sara Bodinson, Associate Educator, David Little, Director of Adult and Academic Programs, and Sarah Ganz, Director, Educational Resources, have ensured that a wide audience of professionals, academics, and laypeople alike have access to the material. Outside the Museum, Pamela Puchalski of The American Institute of Architects; James Fernandez and Laura Turegano of the King Juan Carlos I Center at New York University; and Mark Wigley, Dean, and Benjamin Prosky, Director of Special Events at the Graduate School for Architecture Preservation and Planning at Columbia University, worked closely with MoMA's Department of Education in combining programmatic objectives.

I am extremely fortunate to have had the remarkably competent support of Nobi Nakanishi and Linda Roby, Department Coordinators, in managing an extremely complex schedule and a huge amount of incoming and outgoing communications. Along with Rachel Judlowe, Department Coordinator, they helped to ensure that milestones were reached with punctuality and good humor. Candace Banks, Department Assistant, and Patricia Juncosa Vecchierini, Curatorial Assistant, are also credited with dropping other tasks when asked and lending a hand. Jenny Tobias, Librarian, and independent researcher Elena Juncosa Vecchierini also provided crucial research assistance.

With great tenacity and technical skill, Peter Christensen thoughtfully organized and maintained the information we had assembled, including the hundreds of images that appear in this book and in the exhibition. Peter's hard work and attention to detail is evident not only in this publication, but in the tremendous body of research compiled for this project in its infancy. Alexandra Quantrill deserves further thanks for doggedly pursuing all the complex details related to the thirty-five architectural models that are a hallmark of the exhibition. This research was essential to the accurate advanced planning of the exhibition's production. They have undertaken with good spirits the countless tasks required to complete a project of this nature and they have been devoted to seeing this book and exhibition through to completion, for which I am very grateful.

TERENCE RILEY
THE PHILIP JOHNSON CHIEF CURATOR,
DEPARTMENT OF ARCHITECTURE AND DESIGN

Trustees of The Museum of Modern Art